Inclusive Marriage Services

❦ A WEDDING SOURCEBOOK ❦

Kimberly Bracken Long and David Maxwell, editors

CONTRIBUTORS

Kimberly L. Clayton ❖ David Gambrell
Kimberly Bracken Long ❖ David Maxwell
Ruth A. Meyers ❖ Bradley E. Schmeling

WESTMINSTER JOHN KNOX PRESS
LOUISVILLE · KENTUCKY

© 2015 Westminster John Knox Press

First edition

Published by Westminster John Knox Press
Louisville, Kentucky

16 17 18 19 20 21 22 23 24—10 9 8 7 6 5 4 3 2

Inclusive marriage service from the United Church of Canada is reprinted from *Celebrate God's Presence: A Book of Services* © The United Church of Canada. Used with permission. Within this service, the following are under separate copyright and used by permission: The Opening Prayer, Declaration, and Blessing of the Couple are adapted with permission from the *Book of Worship, United Church of Christ*. Reprinted copyright © 2012 by United Church of Christ, Local Church Ministries, Cleveland, Ohio. © 1986 by United Church of Christ Office for Church Life and Leadership, New York. All rights reserved. Used by permission. The Statement of Purpose and the Blessing of the Couple are reprinted from *Celebrate God's Presence*, United Church of Christ, and originally adapted with permission from *New Zealand Prayer Book: He Karakia Mihinarea a Aotearoa* © The Provincial Secretary, the Church of the Province of New Zealand, Rotorua. William Collins Publishers Ltd., Auckland; the Prayer of Confession, Words of Assurance, and Exchange of Rings © Janet Cawley and used by permission; Promises and Blessings by the Family and by the Community © Jean Ward and Nigel Weaver and used by permission; and Prayer for Illumination from the *Book of Common Worship*, Westminster/John Knox Press (Louisville, KY: 1993), 91. Inclusive marriage service from Uniting Network Australia adapted from *Sacred Union Ceremony: Towards Pastoral and Liturgical Recognition for Gay and Lesbian Couples in the Uniting Church in Australia*, 2010. Compiled by Leanne Jenski, Robert Stringer, Warren Talbot and Susan Wickham. Originally published by the Uniting Network Australia. Prayers taken from the First Order of Marriage from the *Book of Common Order*, published by Saint Andrew Press, copyright © Panel on Worship of the Church of Scotland, 1994, 1996, 2005. "A Hymn in Praise of God's Love" by Michael Morgan is used by permission. All rights reserved. "Rejoice in Christ the Lord! (In Love Abide)" by David Gambrell is used by permission. "From Sacred Love" by Mary Louise Bringle. Copyright © 2002 by GIA Publications, Inc., 7404 S. Mason Ave., Chicago, IL 60638, www.giamusic.com, 800.442.1358. All rights reserved. Used by permission. "Love Has Brought Us Here Together" by Mary Louise Bringle. Copyright © 2010 by GIA Publications, Inc., 7404 S. Mason Ave., Chicago, IL 60638, www.giamusic.com, 800.442.1358. All rights reserved. Used by permission.

Every effort has been made to determine whether texts are under copyright. If through an oversight any copyrighted material has been used without permission, and the publisher is notified of this, acknowledgment will be made in future printings.

Permission is granted to churches to reprint individual prayers and liturgical texts for worship provided it is not under copyright and that the following notice is included: Reprinted by permission of Westminster John Knox Press from *Inclusive Marriage Services*. Copyright 2015.

Book design by Drew Stevens
Cover design by Mark Abrams

Library of Congress Cataloging-in-Publication Data

Inclusive marriage services : a wedding sourcebook / Kimberly Bracken Long and David Maxwell, editors ; contributors, Kimberly L. Clayton, David Gambrell, Kimberly Bracken Long, David Maxwell, Ruth A. Meyers, Bradley E. Schmeling.
  pages cm
  ISBN 978-0-664-26219-8 (hbk. : alk. paper) — ISBN 978-0-664-26031-6 (pbk. : alk. paper) 1. Marriage service. 2. Weddings. I. Long, Kimberly Bracken, editor.
  BV199.M3I53 2016
  265'.5—dc23

                                                              2015022543

∞ The paper used in this publication meets the minimum requirements of the American National Standard for Information Sciences—Permanence of Paper for Printed Library Materials, ANSI Z39.48-1992.

For all who have worked diligently for marriage equality,
and for pastors and couples who strive to reflect
God's wildly inclusive love.

Contents

Hymns

Prayers for Particular Occasions

PART 3. PRACTICAL CONCERNS

Acknowledgments

This book is the product of several gifted writers who have presided at many weddings and listened to the stories of friends, colleagues, parishioners, and strangers. They have been involved in the struggle for marriage equality—some of them in costly and profound ways. As a result, they have thought deeply about the theological, ecclesial, and legal issues related to marriage. Their work is a labor of love.

This work also grows out of the commitment of so many others who have fought for marriage equality in both the legal and ecclesial realms. We are aware of the dedication and tenacity of those people—gay and straight—who have worked for years to ensure that marriage is available to all. This book is dedicated to them.

We are grateful to a number of people who enabled this book to come to fruition. Westminster John Knox Press generously allowed the writers and editors to meet together for a weekend at the beginning of the project. Columbia Theological Seminary provided meeting space. J. Scott Miller contributed additional material. We are particularly appreciative of friends and colleagues around the world who granted permission to include services from their ecclesial bodies.

Finally, we give thanks to our ancestors in the faith who shaped the marriage rites from which these liturgies have grown, with prayers that those who use these services will find them to be faithful to the gospel of Jesus Christ and a source of blessing for their unions.

Introduction

Marriage is not for everybody. Some find fulfillment in singleness, and others choose to avoid the institution for personal or legal reasons. In recent years, however, more people who want to marry are allowed to do so. As same-sex marriage has become legal across the United States, and as more churches welcome same-gender couples and diverse families, more and more Christians are asking for inclusive wedding services.

The inclusive wedding services in this book provide language that can be used by gay and straight couples alike. These marriage rites sound like the church weddings you have heard before; they echo Christian convictions about covenant, commitment, fidelity, and love. They were written by people who treasure their denominational heritages and appreciate good liturgical language. What is different about these services is that the language for couples is not gender specific. There is little emphasis on procreation as a chief purpose for marriage. Some services are appropriate for all kinds of couples, and others are intended for couples who are blending families or who have been together for a long time. This book, then, does not seek to reinvent the wedding or redefine marriage. Readers will find that the services here echo historic marriage rites while using language that is broadly inclusive.

This book is designed to offer complete liturgies, additional liturgical material, and brief essays to guide pastors and couples as they plan weddings. The contributors are:

Kimberly L. Clayton, Decatur, Georgia
David Gambrell, Louisville, Kentucky
Kimberly Bracken Long, Decatur, Georgia
David Maxwell, Louisville, Kentucky
Ruth A. Meyers, Berkeley, California
Bradley E. Schmeling, Saint Paul, Minnesota

Four newly composed inclusive marriage liturgies are included here. While all of the services can be used or adapted for a wide variety of situations, each was written with particular concerns in mind:

— Marriage Liturgy A is for general use, or for couples who are marrying for the first time.
— Marriage Liturgy B is for couples who have been in a long-term, committed relationship.
— Marriage Liturgy C is for couples who have children living at home and are blending families.
— Marriage Liturgy D is for couples in which one partner is not Christian (useful for interfaith couples or those with little or no connection to the church).

Five additional services from ecclesial bodies around the world also appear:

— The order for marriage from the second edition of the United Church of Christ *Book of Worship*
— An adaptation of a wedding service from *Celebrate God's Presence*, the worship book of the United Church of Canada
— An adaptation of a gender-neutral service provided by the Uniting Network Australia, a national network of lesbian, gay, bisexual, transgender, and intersex people working for safety and equality in the Uniting Church in Australia
— An adaptation of the First Order of Marriage found in the *Book of Common Order*, the worship book of the Church of Scotland
— An adaptation of Rite I in the *Book of Common Worship*, the worship book of the Presbyterian Church (U.S.A.)

We are aware that some denominations are already about the work of making their marriage liturgies more inclusive. In the meantime, the services provided here might be useful.

A sourcebook section provides additional prayers, vows, and other liturgical elements that are not found in the complete services. Material from the complete liturgies is also incorporated into this section. In addition, you will find the texts of four wedding hymns with suggested tunes, two of which appear in print for the first time in these pages.

Several short essays on practical questions related to weddings round out the book. Some of these topics—like "Walking Down the Aisle"—are simply meant to help with some of the nitty-gritty details of weddings. Others are meant to advise on more sensitive topics, such as whether or not to include children from previous relationships in the making of promises, or how to address issues related to same-gender couples who are only now able to marry. Finally, Scripture readings are suggested, along with ideas for wedding homilies.

Those planning wedding services can use any of the liturgies as they are presented here; they may use a particular service as a starting point and add or substitute other elements found in the sourcebook section; or they may construct a service using elements from the sourcebook. All of the material provided in the newly composed services also appears in the sourcebook section, as well as material that appears only in the sourcebook. A number of selections taken from the denominational liturgies also appear in the sourcebook.

Several principles guide the work that appears here. First, language of husband and wife, or male and female, is avoided. Sometimes this means that there is more focus on action than on naming a person's role. So then, "I, N., take you, N., to be my loving and faithful wife" might become, "N., my beloved, I give myself to you." In other cases, options are provided, as in "I, N., take you, N., to be my love, my partner, my *spouse/husband/wife*."

Second, the services are designed to be flexible, so they can be adapted to various situations. Between the complete liturgies and the additional prayers, vows, and statements found in the sourcebook, couples will be able to shape their wedding services in ways that give praise to God, express their Christian faith, and reflect the particularity of their families.

Third, vows are at the heart of any wedding service. Although the words of the vows in this book have been carefully chosen to be inclusive, you will notice that they also echo the kinds of vows Christians have been making for centuries. We recognize the power of saying words that have been said by other generations of believers, especially when the right to speak them has been denied to some for so long.

Fourth, you may notice variations in the order of elements in the various services. Since our writers are from different denominations, and because we include services from a variety of traditions, we have chosen to let those differences stand, rather than impose uniformity.

Finally, the sacraments of baptism and Eucharist undergird these services. Marriage is one way—among many—that Christians live out their baptismal vocations. Christians who marry live out the faith in their marriages, practicing the art of mutual self-giving and seeking to forgive one another as Christ has forgiven them. They also live out their faith as a couple, together striving to love and serve God, to show compassion to others, and to work for God's coming realm of justice and peace. Furthermore, when Christians gather around the table, Christ is present as guest and host; we share in a foretaste of the heavenly marriage banquet; we are fed for the journey and strengthened to live out our vocations in all of life, including marriage. Only some of the services here include eucharistic liturgy, but Communion can be celebrated in any of the liturgies, and the sourcebook contains several eucharistic prayers.

It is our hope that one day this book will become obsolete, and all marriage rites will be fully inclusive. Until that day, we pray that the words found here will be helpful and that those who speak these vows will be blessed in their marriages.

PART 1

❧ INCLUSIVE MARRIAGE SERVICES ☙
AND
REAFFIRMATION OF VOWS

Marriage Liturgy A

[This service is for general use.]

OPENING HYMN OR PROCESSIONAL MUSIC

GATHERING

Sisters and brothers,
we are gathered here to celebrate the union of N. and N.,
to witness the vows they make to one another,
to pledge our support and encouragement,
and to seek God's blessing upon their marriage.

God created us for companionship
and gave us the capacity for joy.
Jesus Christ showed us self-giving love
and taught us to continually forgive.
And the Holy Spirit, given in our baptism,
renews grace within us day by day
and enables us to grow in faith, in hope, and in love.

Marriage is a gift and a calling
in which two people become for one another
a source of love,
a fount of blessing,
and a deep well of grace,
bearing each other's burdens
and sharing in each other's joys.

As N. and N. commit their lives to one another,
families are joined,
friendships are forged and strengthened,
and a new community of love is formed.

As we bear witness to the vows being made today,
let us surround N. and N. with affection and prayer,
giving thanks for all the ways
that God's love is made manifest in our lives.

DECLARATION OF INTENT
[Asked in turn to each person]
N., do you freely choose N.
and intend to enter the covenant of marriage?
I do.

AFFIRMATION OF FAMILY AND FRIENDS
Do all of you, the family and friends of N. and N.,
pledge to uphold them in their marriage
and encourage them in their life together?
We do.

PRAYER
God of life and love,
thank you for leading N. and N. to one another,
for planting in them the seeds of mutual love,
and bringing them to this day of promise making.

We love because you first loved us;
we dare to make vows because
you have made a covenant with us.
In Jesus Christ, you showed us how to give of ourselves to others
and taught us how to forgive.

Shine your light on us today,
and especially upon N. and N.,
as they bind themselves to one another.
By your Spirit may they know the promise of your deep and
    abiding love
this day, and through all the days to come.
In Jesus' name we pray. **Amen.**

READINGS FROM SCRIPTURE

SERMON

[A hymn may be sung.]

VOWS

A

N., I give myself to you.
Through joys and sorrows,
triumphs and troubles,
in times of plenty and times of want,
I will remain faithful to you
and love you through all of our days.

B

N., I bind myself to you this day
and promise to love you and cherish you,
to support you and comfort you,
to honor you and keep faith with you
as long as we both shall live.

EXCHANGE OF RINGS

N., I give you this ring
as a sign of our unending love
and abiding trust.

PRAYER

Eternal God,
we give you thanks for all the ways you fill our lives with love,
and especially for the love you have given to N. and N.
Bless them in their life together,
that their love for one another may deepen
and their trust in you may grow.

Give them wisdom in their common life
and nurture in them the gift of your grace,
that together they may learn
to love with an everlasting love.

When they hurt one another,
enable them to show mercy.
Cultivate in them a habit of forgiveness,
and lead them into ever-deepening and mutual self-giving.
Teach them to honor one another in all things
and enable them to keep the vows they have made this day
through whatever joys they share or troubles that befall them.

May this marriage be a gift to all who know N. and N.
Make their life together an expression of your own love for this world,
that in their esteem for one another,
their relationships with neighbors,
and their service to those in need,
all who know them will see a glimpse of your coming reign
of justice, peace, and love.

Bless those gathered here today,
that all who witness these vows
may find their hope renewed
and know the depth of your love and care
for them and for this world you cherish.
All praise to you, triune God,
who created us for love,
became love for the world,
and nurtures love in us all. **Amen.**

DECLARATION OF MARRIAGE

N. and N. have made promises to one another
in the presence of God and this assembly
and have sealed those promises with the giving and
    receiving of rings.
Let their marriage be held in honor by all.

CHARGE

Let love be genuine;   *Rom. 12:9–13, 18*
hate what is evil, hold fast to what is good;
love one another with mutual affection;
outdo one another in showing honor.
Do not lag in zeal, be ardent in spirit, serve the Lord.

Rejoice in hope,
be patient in suffering,
persevere in prayer.
Contribute to the needs of the saints;
extend hospitality to strangers.
If it is possible, so far as it depends on you,
live peaceably with all.

BLESSING

May the grace of Christ attend you,
the love of God surround you,
and the Holy Spirit keep you,
this day and forevermore. **Amen.**

[The couple may seal their vows with a kiss.]

SENDING HYMN OR RECESSIONAL MUSIC

Marriage Liturgy B

[This service is well suited for those who have been in a long-term committed relationship. It includes the celebration of Communion.]

GREETING

This is the day our God has made.
Let us rejoice and be glad in it.

May the faithfulness of God,
the presence of Christ,
and the life of the Holy Spirit
be with you all.
And also with you.

AFFIRMATION OF MARRIAGE

Beloved, love is from God.
Everyone who loves is born of God and knows God.
At the beginning of time, God said that it was not good to be alone
and created us to be in relationship with others.
Made in the image of God,
we are given the capacity to love and be loved.
The making of promises is a sacramental sign
of God's faithfulness and intention for the whole creation.

God blesses those who love one another
and promises to be an ever-present source of strength
for those who build a life together.
On this day, we gather as a community of friends
to witness this new step in N. and N.'s journey.

We recognize that the support of community is essential,
and we give thanks that we can offer our prayers,
our solidarity,
and our friendship to N. and N. for their life together.

CALL TO CONFESSION

God desires that all creation might be one;
that love be central to human life;
and that all may know peace and mercy.
Trusting in God's mercy,
let us come before God to confess that sin has often
broken our relationships and brought pain to the creation.

PRAYER OF CONFESSION

**Gracious God,
we have not always followed your command
to fill the earth with blessing.
We have hurt the people we love the most;
we have shown little concern for those we do not know.
Our society has created barriers and sent minorities to the margins.
Our church has not offered its blessing as Christ commanded us.**

**Forgive us, and give us strength to right the wrongs of the past.
Open our hearts to your ever-widening love,
and make us advocates for justice.
Bind our hearts to the forgiveness that you offer,
and let us never tire of practicing mercy.
In Jesus' name we pray. Amen.**

DECLARATION OF FORGIVENESS

God never turns from us,
but works within the creation to bring us home.
The forgiveness that God offers in Jesus Christ is yours.
Heaven rejoices when all are gathered into joyful celebration.
Enter this joy, and be at peace,
now and forever. **Amen.**

STATEMENT OF INTENT

N., you have shared your life with N. for these last ___ years.
Do you intend to continue in this relationship,
to mature in love,
deepen in faith,
and grow in compassion?
Will you carry forward the best of what you bring to one another,
and continue to work on those things with which you struggle,
honoring the work God has accomplished with you?
I will, and I ask God to help me.

AFFIRMATION OF FAMILY AND FRIENDS

Do you, the family and friends of N. and N.,
promise to encourage them in their marriage,
share in their joy,
and offer your best support and prayers?
We do, and we ask God to help us.

PRAYER OF THE DAY

God of wonder and delight,
When you crafted human beings with your own hands
and breathed into them the breath of life,
you set into motion a love that would shape all of history.
Breathe that same spirit into this marriage between N. and N.

You have provided for them since the beginning;
now give them courage to make their promises,
and the creativity to keep them,
until that day when you gather us all into the celebration
that will have no end.
In Jesus' name we pray. **Amen.**

[A hymn of praise may be sung.]

PRAYER FOR ILLUMINATION

Gracious God,
you inspired faithful people to write of your love.
Your Scriptures proclaim the ever-widening call
to love one another and to cherish created life.

Open our ears to the sound of your voice,
that we might hear of your unending faithfulness
and your promise to carry us safely into eternal life,
bound together forever
in the love of Jesus Christ. **Amen.**

READINGS FROM SCRIPTURE

SERMON

[A hymn may be sung.]

VOWS

N. and N.,
now join hands,
and make your promises to one another.

I, N., promise to love you with my whole heart,
with my imagination, and with my body.
In all things, I promise to understand,
to forgive,
and to take delight in you.
I will keep these promises on good days and on bad,
when I'm confident and when I'm afraid,
when our life together is joyful,
and when our life is difficult.
As I have from the beginning of our relationship,
I will give myself to you with humility and with passion
all the days of our lives.

BLESSING OF RINGS

Bless the rings that these hands have worn
these last ___ years.
May they continue to be a visible sign
of their faithfulness,
a circle of eternal love
adorning their daily life. **Amen.**

[Each spouse will say:]
I wear this ring as an everlasting sign
of my love and faithfulness.

ACCLAMATION

Having made their promises before God and this assembly
and given public witness to their commitment,
N. and N. are now married in the state of ___ [in the eyes of God and
the church].
Those whom God has brought together, let no one separate.
Thanks be to God.

*[Other signs of marriage may be used at this time. If the marriage certificate
is signed during the ceremony, it may be done at this point.]*

MARRIAGE BLESSING

*[The minister may lay hands on the heads of the couple. In addition, the
assembly may gather around for the laying on of hands.]*
Pour out your Holy Spirit on N. and N.
Continue to give them strength
to live together with love and compassion.
Fill them with genuine delight in one another.
Give them enough creativity to overcome their challenges,
and enough humility to forgive their mistakes.
Grant them patience and generosity,
compassion and tenderness.
Bless their home and make it a place of peace and justice.
Bring your blessing to their waking and sleeping,
to their work and to their play,
to their family and to their friends.

And, at the last, bring them into your eternal home
where all promises will be fulfilled, all wounds healed,
and all gathered in love forever,
through Jesus Christ, our Savior and Light. **Amen.**

*[Prayers of intercession may be included here. Each petition may end with the
words, "God of mercy, **Send us your love.**"]*

*[If Communion is being celebrated, the service continues with the peace. If
there is no Communion, the service continues with the final blessing.]*

SHARING THE PEACE OF CHRIST

The peace of Christ be with you always.
And also with you.

[The assembly may greet one another with a sign of peace.]

SETTING THE TABLE

[An offering may be collected for the work of the church or to support a cause that is important to the couple. Bread and wine may be set on the table and Communion prepared.]

PRAYER OF GREAT THANKSGIVING

The Lord be with you.
And also with you.
Lift up your hearts.
We lift them to the Lord.
Let us give thanks to the Lord our God.
It is right to give our thanks and praise.

It is indeed right, our duty and our joy,
that we should at all times and all places
give our thanks and praise to you, gracious God,
through our Savior Jesus Christ.
At the wedding in Cana in Galilee
Jesus turned water into wine,
making marriage a sign of a glory that is yet to come.
With great joy, with our whole lives,
and with all the saints,
we praise your name and join their unending hymn:

Holy, holy, holy Lord, God of power and might,
heaven and earth are full of your glory.
Hosanna in the highest.
Blessed is the one who comes in the name of the Lord.
Hosanna in the highest.

Holy mystery,
energy that powers the universe,
your Word set creation into motion:
ever-expanding, evolving, multiplying, flourishing.

You brought human life out of primordial mist,
setting us in this garden home,
instilling in us the capacity to love,
endowing us with the imagination
to form friendships and make love.
We heard you tell our ancient parents
that it is not good to be alone
and command them to fill the earth with blessing.

Yet, so often, we were afraid.
We failed to nurture your good creation.
We limited the wideness of your love
by pretending that some are loved by you,
and others are outside your grace.
Again and again, you sent men to remind us of mercy,
and women to demand justice.

At the right time, you sent Jesus,
an open channel of light and love,
who turned water into wine,
rejection into welcome,
hunger into fullness,
and death into life.

On the night after a woman
anointed his feet with perfumed oil,
the night of his own suffering and betrayal,
Jesus gathered with friends and washed their feet.
He took bread, gave thanks, broke it,
and gave it to them, saying:
Take and eat; this is my body, given for you.
We do this to remember that we are his body.

After the meal, he took a cup of wine,
gave thanks, and shared it for all to drink, saying:
This cup is the sign of a new covenant,
offered to the whole creation
that sins might be forgiven
and love restored.
We do this to remember that we share his life.

Remembering his promise to be present
whenever we gather at this table,
let us proclaim the mystery of faith:
Christ has died.
Christ is risen.
Christ will come again.

At this table
pour out your gentle Spirit,
turning this marriage celebration into heaven,
this bread and wine into holy food,
and this assembly into a community of love that never ends.
Amen. Come, Holy Spirit.

To you, Holy God,
our source, our light,
our bread, our life,
our water and our wine,
we give you praise,
without reserve,
without end. **Amen.**

Gathered by the Holy Spirit, let us pray as Jesus taught us.

[The assembly prays the Lord's Prayer.]

BREAKING OF THE BREAD
Reveal yourself to us in the breaking of the bread,
as you once revealed yourself to the disciples.

Make this cup a sign of great celebration
as when you once turned water into wine.

These are the gifts of God for the people of God.
Thanks be to God.

COMMUNION OF THE PEOPLE

PRAYER AFTER COMMUNION

Jesus Christ,
friend and lover,
we give you thanks for joining us in this celebration.
Now that we have feasted on your glory
and have known your mercy,
pour us out for the sake of the world,
that all might know this love
and be drawn into a community of justice. **Amen.**

BLESSING

The God of creation,
who made you and delights in you;
the Christ of incarnation,
who redeemed you and befriends you;
the Spirit of power,
who gives you life and passion;
bless you now and for the rest of your days. **Amen.**

As a testimony to your promises and your love
you may kiss one another.

DISMISSAL

Go forth in peace and joy.
Thanks be to God.

Marriage Liturgy C

[This service is appropriate for a couple with children who are living at home.]

GREETING

    We gather to worship God,
    whose love is abounding and steadfast,   *Exod. 34:6*
    whose faithfulness never comes to an end.
    As the family and friends of N. and N.,
    we gather to witness their vows to one another,
    celebrate the promises they make this day,
    and surround them with our prayers,
    that their love may grow
    and all creation may flourish with new life.

OPENING SENTENCES

    How very good and pleasant it is   *Ps. 133*
    when kindred live together in unity!
    It is like precious oil on the head,
    running down the beard of Aaron,
    running down over the collar of his robes.
    It is like the dew of Hermon,
    which falls on the mountains of Zion.
    For there the Lord ordained blessing,
    life forevermore.

[A hymn may be sung.]

STATEMENT ON THE GIFT OF MARRIAGE

Beloved Community,
God has created us to be in relationship with the Divine,
with other people,
and with all creation.
Christian marriage is a visible sign
of unity in a broken world
and a covenant call to faithfulness.
In Christian marriage,
two people commit to a way of life together
that is marked by love, joy, peace,   *Gal. 5:22–23*
patience, kindness, generosity, and self-control—
gifts of the Holy Spirit
available to all.
Marriage can be a haven from the storms of life,
a place of refuge and lodging;
and it is also an invitation
to reach out in wide and generous welcome
to stranger, and neighbor, and friend.
Into this estate,
N. and N. come now to be joined.

PRAYER

Gracious God, your glory shines.   *Isa. 60:1, 5*
We see your radiance,
and our hearts rejoice.
You have given us gift upon gift
until we are filled with gratitude.
Now we thank you for the way love comes to us,
like grace,
immeasurable, unearned.
Especially we thank you for the love
that N. and N. have come to profess.
Bless the promises they will make this day.
Strengthen them in their life together.
Be to us all an everlasting light   *Isa. 60:19c, 21b*
and make us the work of your own hands—
all for your glory.
In Christ's name, we pray. **Amen.**

CALL TO CONFESSION

The God of grace,
who knows our inmost thoughts
and sees our failings,
waits in mercy to forgive.
In faith, let us confess our sin
before God and one another.

PRAYER OF CONFESSION

Merciful God,
we fail to live by your Word
and do not keep faith with you or one another.
Take the promises
that lie broken on the floors of our lives;
sweep them away,
or make of the shards a new design.
Turn us back to you
until good intentions
become deeds of justice and love.
To turn will be our delight,
for in turning,
we return
to you and to one another,
a new creation in Jesus Christ,   *2 Cor. 5:17*
through whom we pray. Amen.

ASSURANCE OF PARDON

Friends,
forgiveness comes from God,   *2 Cor. 5:19–20*
who is not counting our trespasses against us.
For God has reconciled us through Christ,
and entrusts to us the message of reconciliation.
We are ambassadors for Christ,
sharing his peace with all.
The peace of the Lord Jesus Christ be with you.
And also with you.

[The people may exchange signs of peace with one another.]

DECLARATION OF INTENT

[Asked in turn to each person]
N., is it your heart's desire and true intent
to enter into the covenant of marriage,
giving of yourself in every way,
with mutual love and respect?
This is my desire and intent.

AFFIRMATION OF FAMILY AND FRIENDS

Friends and family gathered here,
do you promise to support N. and N.,
as they build a family together?
We do.

PRAYER FOR ILLUMINATION

Almighty God,
illumine our hearts and minds
as your word is read and proclaimed,
so that, by the power of your Holy Spirit,
we may respond in faith.
Perfect your love in us   *1 John 4:16–17*
so that we may abide in you
and love others boldly in your name. **Amen.**

SCRIPTURE READING(S)

SERMON

EXCHANGE OF VOWS

I, N., take you, N.,
to be my love, my partner, my *spouse/husband/wife*;
and I promise
to dwell with you in faithfulness;
to live in the spirit of mutuality,
and to share equally in our common life.
I will support you in times of struggle
and share your deepest hopes
to our life's end.

QUESTION TO THE COUPLE REGARDING CHILDREN

N. and N., your life together is blessed by children.
Just as you make vows to one another,
you also make promises to your children.

[Have the couple and the children face one another. If the children are sitting in the congregation, have them stand. Have each parent repeat these words to the children of the other parent.]

[Name the children],
Like you, I love your *mother/father* very much.
As I promise to love, respect, and honor *her/him*,
I also promise to love, respect, and honor you.
May our lives together reflect God's love and forgiveness,
and may our home be filled with peace, laughter, and much joy.

QUESTION FOR THE CHILDREN (IF THEY ARE OLDER)

[Name the children], your parent(s) seek(s) to build a home
where you are loved in joy and safety;
where you grow in ways that honor your life and gifts;
and where mutual respect is given and received.
Will you do all you can to contribute
to the well-being of this family
as your parent(s) enter(s) into marriage this day?
***I/We* will.**

QUESTION FOR THE CHILDREN (IF THEY ARE YOUNGER)

[Name the children], your parent(s) love(s) you
and want(s) you to be at home in this new family.
Together, they will do all they can to help you grow,
in good times and in hard times.
Do you promise to love them, too,
in good times and in hard times,
as you grow together as a family?
***I/We* do.**

EXCHANGE OF RINGS

[The presider may say the following prayer.]
God of steadfast love,
you have given us signs
by which we remember your covenants:

the rainbow,
the stars in the night sky.
In this covenant of marriage,
we bring these rings;
made of strong metals from the earth,
they bend and join,
forming a circle.
Bless these rings, we pray,
that they may be to N. and N.
symbols of the promises
they make this day.
May the strength and humility
of their mutual love
bind and bend them
toward each other,
now and always. **Amen.**

[*Each says to the other as the ring is given:*]
This ring I give you
as gift and symbol
of our union in marriage,
and of the greater circle of love
in which we are forever known,
and held,
and remembered of God.

DECLARATION OF MARRIAGE

By the vows made this day
in the presence of God and this community,
I declare that N. and N.
are now joined in the covenant of marriage.
In the household of faith,
we rejoice with them and their children
on this glad occasion,
and celebrate with joy
their life together.

PRAYER

Gracious God,
because you first loved us,
we are able to love one another.

We thank you for this great gift
that makes all of life deeper, richer,
and more colorful than it might otherwise have been.
We thank you for those who have supported us
and helped us to mature
so that we might be ready for new responsibilities and new
   opportunities.
We remember today those who are not present among us,
and trust that in your great care and keeping,
there is a wider circle of mercy and love
than we ourselves can draw.

We ask, dear God,
that you will especially tend and nurture N. and N.
as they begin their married life this day
and that they, with their children [*names of the children may be said*]
will grow in joy and peace and hope.
In their household,
let kindness and gentleness mark their days.
Give them the spirit of forgiveness and patience;
and may joy and laughter be ready companions through the years.
Give them more companions besides—
those who will rejoice or weep with them,
those whose love will be steadfast and sure.

Bless all who have worshiped this day,
that their lives may also be strengthened
for love and by love.
Teach us to recognize
the abundance of all you so freely offer,
so that we may become more generous in a world of need.
Make us lovers and reconcilers and peacemakers,
ambassadors of all your wide and wild purposes.
Because you have welcomed us into your own household,
we, too, will open the doors of our hearts and homes
until your kingdom comes.
In Christ's name, we pray. **Amen.**

[*A hymn may be sung.*]

CHARGE

The commandment we have had from God   *2 John 5–6*
from the beginning is this:
let us love one another.
And this is love:
that we walk according to God's word and ways.
As we go from this place,
where love has been promised, professed, and sealed,
let us practice love
steadfastly and abundantly!

BENEDICTION

The love of God,
the grace of Christ,
and the peace of the Holy Spirit
fill you this day
and forever.

Marriage Liturgy D

*[This service may be helpful for a couple in one of the following situations:
(a) one or both of the partners is not an actively practicing Christian; (b) it
is an interfaith marriage; (c) the wedding will take place outside of a church
and the presider is a family friend, college or hospital chaplain, or the like.
This service strikes a careful balance by offering words that both presider
and couple can say with integrity. This is a Christian service that includes
biblical language and prayer, yet is broadly inclusive of those who may not be
Christian.]*

A SERVICE OF MARRIAGE

*[As the people gather, appropriate music may be offered to the glory of
God. The couple and other members of the wedding party enter and stand
before the minister.]*

WORDS OF WELCOME

A

Let us love one another, for love is from God.   *1 John 4:7*
All those who have love are children of God.

B

Now, beloved, put on the garment of love,   *Col. 3:14*
for love binds all things together in harmony.

C

Faith, hope, and love abide, these three;   *1 Cor. 13:13*
and the greatest of these is love.
Let us worship God.

[A hymn may be sung.]

WORDS OF PURPOSE
We gather here, in God's presence,
to witness the marriage of N. and N.,
surrounding them with our joy,
embracing them with our support,
and upholding them in our prayers.
Marriage is a gift from God—
the gift of love between two people
who promise to care for one another
and be faithful in the love they share.
Marriage is a new way of life—
the joining together of two people
who promise to seek the common good
and reach out with love to others.

[The minister asks the couple:]
A
N., do you now desire
to give yourself to N. in marriage?
I do.

B
N., do you now desire
to share your life with N. in marriage?
I do.

[The minister asks the families:]
Do you, the families of N. and N.,
promise to support and surround them
with your faith, hope, and love?
We do.

[The minister asks the people:]
Do you, the friends of N. and N.,
promise to help and encourage them
in their new life together?
We do.

WORDS OF SCRIPTURE

Let us pray.
Holy God, now send your Spirit
to open our hearts and minds
to the story of your steadfast love for all.
May these words of promise and hope
take root, and grow, and bear good fruit
in the hearts and lives of N. and N.,
and in all of us gathered here,
so that our lives may be made new
by the power of your living Word. **Amen.**

[Appropriate passages of Scripture may be read.]

[A brief sermon proclaims the good news of God's saving love and the calling to love one another.]

[A hymn may be sung.]

WORDS OF PROMISE

[The couple exchange their vows:]

A
N., my beloved,
I give myself to you—
heart and mind,
body and soul,
now and always.

B
With you, N.,
I will share my life—
all that I am,
all that I have been,
all that I will become.
This I promise.

[If rings are exchanged, they say:]
N., to you
I give this ring:

**sign of promise,
gift of love.**

WORDS OF PRAYER

[The couple join hands and the minister prays:]
Wise and loving God, by your providence
you have brought N. and N. together.
Now, in the mystery of your grace,
let them be united as one.
Let the life they now share
be a sign of your new creation,
a source of new and abundant life,
and a gift of love for all the world;
in your holy name we pray. **Amen.**

[The minister announces the marriage:]
N. and N., you are now married.
Let all that you do be done in love.   *1 Cor. 16:14*

[The couple may kiss.]

[A hymn may be sung.]

WORDS OF BLESSING

[The minister offers a blessing to the couple:]

A
May the Holy and Eternal One—   *Rev. 4:8*
who was and is and is to come—
bless and keep you, now and always.

B
May the One who makes all things new   *Rev. 21:5, 22–27*
write your names in the book of life
and shine on you with endless light.

C
May the God of every blessing   *1 Cor. 13:13*
keep you in faith, hope, and love,
today, tomorrow, and forever.

Church of Scotland

A

God is love;
and those who dwell in love are dwelling in God,
and God is in them.

B

Grace and peace to you from God our Father
and the Lord Jesus Christ.

Let us worship God.

STATEMENT

We have come together in the presence of God,
for the marriage of N. and N.;
to share their joy, and to promise them our support and love.

Marriage is a gift of God
and a means of grace.
In the lifelong union of marriage
we can know the joy of God,
in whose image we are made.

Marriage is founded in God's loving nature,
and in God's covenant of love with us in Christ.
Two people,
in giving themselves to each other in love,
reflect the love of Christ for his church.

When Christians marry
they are called
to live faithfully together,
to love each other with respect,
tenderness, and delight.

They share the life of a home
[and may be trusted
with the gift and care of children].
They help to shape a society
in which human dignity and happiness
may flourish and abound.

Our Lord Jesus Christ was himself
a guest at a wedding in Cana of Galilee.
Through his Spirit he is with us now,
to enrich our love
and to give us his peace and joy.

PRAYERS

Let us pray.
Gracious God,
we thank you for all the gifts of your love,
and especially for the gift of marriage.

We praise you for your guidance
in the lives of N. and N.,
for the joy they find in each other,
and for the love and trust they bring
to the happiness of this day.

And since we know that without you
nothing is strong, nothing is holy,
we pray that you will enrich them
with your grace
as they make their marriage covenant together.
Grant that your joy may be in them,
and that their joy may be full;
through Jesus Christ our Lord. **Amen.**

EXCHANGE OF VOWS

[The congregation standing, the minister says to the couple:]
As a seal to the vows you are about to make,
will you join hands.

In the presence of God
and before these witnesses,
I, N.,
give myself to you, N.
I promise to love you,
to be faithful and loyal to you,
for as long as we live.

[Alternatively, the vows may be put in the form of a question:]
In the presence of God
and before these witnesses,
do you, N., give yourself to N.?
Do you promise to love *her/him*,
to be faithful and loyal to *her/him*,
for as long as you both shall live?
I do.

GIVING AND RECEIVING OF THE RING(S)

[The minister receives the ring(s) and says:]
As a token of the covenant
into which you have entered,
this ring [these rings]
is [are] given and received.
May it [they] be a sign of the unending love
you have pledged to each other this day.

N., I give you this ring in God's name,
as a symbol of all that we have promised,
and all that we shall share.

By this sign you take each other,
to have and to hold from this day forward;
for better, for worse,
for richer, for poorer,

in sickness and in health,
to love and to cherish,
for as long as you live.

DECLARATION OF MARRIAGE
Since you have covenanted together in marriage,
and have declared your love for each other
before God and these witnesses,
I proclaim you to be married
in the name of the Father, and of the Son,
and of the Holy Spirit. **Amen**.

Those whom God has joined together,
no one must separate.

MARRIAGE BLESSING
May the Lord bless you
and guard you;
may the Lord make his face shine on you
and be gracious to you;
may the Lord look kindly on you
and give you peace. **Amen**.

*[The marriage certificate may be signed here, in front of the congregation, or
at the end of the service.]*

HYMN

SCRIPTURE LESSONS, INCLUDING A GOSPEL READING

SERMON

PRAYERS
Let us pray.

Almighty God,
we thank you for all the ways
love comes into our lives,
and for the opportunities of joy and fulfilment
that marriage brings.

Bless N. and N.,
who have been joined together in your name.
Confirm them in their happiness;
keep them faithful and true to each other,
ready to forgive and be forgiven.
As they grow together in love,
may each be to the other
a companion in joy,
a comfort in sorrow,
and a strength in need.

May your presence in their home
make it a place of welcome and sharing,
of security and peace.
[Bless them with the gift and care of children,
that together they may grow
to know and love you in your Son.]

Bless their families and friends,
who have given them love and friendship
through the years.

We pray for your whole human family,
and for those who suffer while we rejoice.
Bring near the day when all people
will live in peace
and in the knowledge of your love.

Eternal God,
we remember those who were close to us,
who have passed through death
into life everlasting.
Bring us with them at the last
to the Father's house,
the family of God complete
in the glory of your presence;
through Jesus Christ our Lord. **Amen**.

[The people may join in praying the Lord's Prayer.]

HYMN

BLESSING
> Go in peace, and in the joy of the Lord.
> And the blessing of God Almighty,
> the Father, the Son, and the Holy Spirit,
> be with you all. **Amen.**

The Uniting Network Australia

[This is a nongender version of the Uniting Church in Australia marriage service prepared by the Uniting Network Australia, a national network of lesbian, gay, bisexual, transgender, and intersex people, and their families and friends. Adapted for use here.]

Marriage is a gift of God
and a means of grace.
In the lifelong union of marriage
we can know the joy of God,
in whose image we are made.

Marriage is founded in God's loving nature,
and in the covenant of love made with us in Christ.
Two partners,
in giving themselves to each other in love,
reflect the love of Christ for his church.

In Christian marriage,
each person is called
to live together faithfully,
and to love the other with respect,
tenderness, and delight.
The companionship and comfort of marriage
enables the full expression
of physical love between the two partners.

They share the life of a home
and may be entrusted
with the gift and care of children.

They help to shape a society
in which human dignity and happiness
may flourish and abound.

Marriage is a way of life that all people should honour;
it is not to be entered into lightly or selfishly,
but responsibly and in the love of God.

N. and N. are now to begin this way of life
that God has created and Christ has blessed.
Therefore, on this their wedding day,
we pray that they may fulfil God's purpose
for the whole of their lives.

[The two covenanters and their attendants may sit.]

SCRIPTURE READINGS

WITNESS/SERMON

HYMN/SONG

DECLARATION OF INTENT
[The person presiding invites the couple to stand together.]
N. and N., do you believe that God has blessed and guided you,
and today calls you into union?
We do.

N., will you give yourself to N. to be *her/his* partner,
to live together in the covenant of union?
Will you love *her/him*, comfort *her/him*,
honour and protect *her/him*, and, forsaking all others,
be faithful to *her/him*, as long as you both shall live?
I will.

AFFIRMATION OF FAMILY AND FRIENDS
[This question can be directed to the parents or immediate family or any individuals or groups that the couple wish to include.]
It is wonderful that you have all gathered here to celebrate this sacred
union between N. and N.

I have asked them some important questions and now it is your turn.
Your response is (I hope) "We do."

Will you, the family and friends of N. and N.,
give your blessing to this sacred union,
and do you promise to uphold them in their journey together?
We do.

PROMISES AND VOWS

*[The word "partner" may be replaced with wife, husband, spouse, or any
other appropriate term. The couple may choose to write or find their own
vows, but the vows must include the promise that this is a lifelong commitment, with words such as "as long as we both shall live" or "until death
parts us."]*

A
I, N., take you, N., to be my partner.
All that I am I give to you,
and all that I have I share with you.
Whatever the future holds,
for better, for worse,
for richer, for poorer,
in sickness and in health,
I will love you and stand by you
as long as we both shall live.

B
I, N., take you, N., to be my partner.
All that I am I give to you,
and all that I have I share with you.
Whatever the future holds,
whether sickness or health,
poverty or prosperity,
conflict or harmony,
I will love you and stand by you
as long as we both shall live.
This is my solemn promise.

C

I, N., offer myself to you, N.,
to be your friend, your lover,
your lifelong companion;
to share my life with yours;
to build our dreams together;
to support you through times of trouble,
and rejoice with you in times of happiness.
I promise to treat you with respect, love, and loyalty
through all the trials and triumphs
of our lives together.
This commitment is made in love,
kept in faith, lived in hope,
and eternally made new.

D

I, N., take you, N.,
to be my partner in life and my one true love.
I will cherish our sacred union
and love you more each day
than I did the day before.
I will trust you and respect you,
laugh with you and cry with you;
loving you faithfully
through good times and bad,
regardless of the obstacles
we may face together.
I give you my hand, and my love
from this day forward
for as long as we both shall live.

E

I, N., take you, N., to be my partner.
Today I promise that I will seek to be there for you
and for us, always:
to create, to live life fully,
to encourage, and to share.
I promise to work with you for common goals,
to walk hand in hand along the paths life will unfold for us,

to create a relationship that
will weather any storms that may come our way,
to communicate openly and honestly, and
to love you faithfully,
as long as we both shall live.
This is my solemn vow.

F
I take you, N., to be my partner;
to laugh with you in joy;
to grieve with you in sorrow;
to grow with you in love;
serving humankind in peace and hope;
as long as we both shall live.

G
From this day forward, I choose you, N.,
to be my *wife/husband* in life;
to live with you and laugh with you,
to stand by your side and sleep in your arms;
to be joy to your heart and food to your soul;
to bring out the best in you always;
and for you, to be the most that I can.
To laugh with you in the good times;
to struggle with you in the bad;
to solace you when you are downhearted;
to share with you all my riches and honours;
to play with you even as we grow old.
I make these promises to you in love,
and until death parts us.

H
I, N., take you, N., to be my partner.
And these things I promise you:
I will be faithful to you with my whole life,
I will be honest with you,
I will respect, trust, help, and care for you,
I will share my life with you,
I will forgive and strengthen you,
and I will grow, with you,

so that we may better understand ourselves,
each other, and the world.
Through the best and worst of what is to come . . .
I make these promises to you, now, and for all our lives.

EXCHANGE OF RINGS
[Prayer over the rings:]
God of steadfast love, by your blessing,
let these rings be to N. and N. a symbol of the vows
that they have made today.
Through Jesus Christ our Lord. Amen.

N., I give you this ring
as a sign of our sacred union
and of the vows that we have made today.

PROCLAMATION
[The couple join hands and the person presiding asks the people to stand and says:]
The Epistle to the Colossians says:
"Above all,
clothe yourselves in love,
which binds everything together
in perfect harmony."

Before the God who is Love,
and in the presence of us all:
N. and N. have made their solemn vows.

They have confirmed their union of covenantal love
by the joining of hands
and in the giving and receiving of rings.

In the name of the triune [One] God
who created all in God's image,
redeems us in Christ Jesus,
and sustains us in the Holy Spirit.

KISS

SIGNING OF REGISTER

PASTORAL PRAYERS

God in your love, hear our prayer.
Bless N. and N. as they begin a new way of life together
as a committed couple in sacred union.
May they be patient and gentle with each other
and ready to face together the challenges of the future.
Be with them in their happiness
and strength in their time of trouble.
Give N. and N. grace when they hurt each other
to acknowledge their fault,
to ask each other's forgiveness,
and to know your love and grace.

May your peace dwell in their home.

[If appropriate] May they enjoy the gift of children
and may they be wise and loving parents.

Bless the parents and families of N. and N.
that they may be united in love and friendship.

May all who have witnessed these vows today
find their lives strengthened
and their relationships renewed.

May each of us be strengthened in our commitment
to care for each other with warmth and love,
to care for those in need with justice and equity,
to care for our planet with integrity and vision.

God, in your love,
Hear our prayer. **Amen.**

BLESSING

The riches of God's grace be upon you,
that you may live together in faith and love
and receive the blessings of eternal life.

May Almighty God,
who creates you, redeems you, and guides you,
bless you now and always. **Amen.**

ANNOUNCEMENT OF THE UNION
[The person presiding asks the people to stand and says:]
And, now I invite all of you to be among the first to welcome N. and N.
as partners in life and love through this sacred union.

United Church of Canada

From *Celebrate God's Presence**

GATHERING

PROCESSIONAL MUSIC

ENTRY

[The couple and their attendants may gather at the front of the sanctuary with the presider.]

GREETING

On behalf of all the people of N. Church
I welcome you, and especially N. and N.
[and their child(ren) N. (and N.)].

OPENING PRAYER

Let us pray.
O God, we gather to celebrate
the gift of your love which is present among us.

---

* The Opening Prayer, Declaration, and Blessing of the Couple are adapted with permission from *Book of Worship*, United Church of Christ. Reprinted copyright © 2012 by United Church of Christ, Local Church Ministries, Cleveland, Ohio. © 1986 by United Church of Christ Office for Church Life and Leadership, New York. All rights reserved. Used by permission. The Statement of Purpose and the Blessing of the Couple are reprinted from *Celebrate God's Presence*, United Church of Christ, and originally adapted with permission from *New Zealand Prayer Book: He Karakia Mihinarea a Aotearoa* © The Provincial Secretary, the Church of the Province of New Zealand, Rotorua. William Collins Publishers Ltd., Auckland. The Prayer of Confession, Words of Assurance, and Exchange of Rings © Janet Cawley and used by permission. Promises and Blessings by the Family and by the Community © Jean Ward and Nigel Weaver and used by permission. Prayer for Illumination from the *Book of Common Worship*, Westminster/John Knox Press (Louisville, KY: 1993), 91.

We rejoice that N. and N. have chosen
to commit themselves to a life of loving faithfulness
[We give you thanks for their child(ren)
who already enrich(es) the love N. and N. share.]
We praise you, O God,
for the ways you have touched our lives
with a variety of loving relationships,
and we give thanks that we know
the life and giving love of Jesus,
in loving and being loved by others. Amen.

STATEMENT OF PURPOSE
We have gathered to celebrate
the marriage of N. and N.
A covenant of lifelong fidelity is the promise of hope
between two people who love each other,
who trust that love, and who wish to share the future together.

Such a covenant enables two people
to share their desires, longings, dreams, and memories,
and to help each other through their uncertainties.
It provides the encouragement
to commit more and more deeply to one another.
[United as one, the two may provide the love and support
in which children grow and flourish.]

Here in the presence of God
we affirm N. and N. in their relationship
as they begin their covenanted union with each other
[accompanied by their child(ren)].

MUSIC

PRAYER OF CONFESSION
Love is not always easy.
Loving one another requires patience, faith, strength, and hope.
Often we make mistakes,
failing to live up to our visions and God's hopes.
Let us come before God in confession.

God of love,
in the warmth of your presence,
and in the warmth of the love celebrated here today,
we confess our failures to love.
We love ourselves,
but not enough to honour your image in us.
We love others,
but not enough to always be patient, gentle, and kind.
Forgive us.
Lead us in your way
that we may truly and rightly love you,
ourselves, and others. Amen.

WORDS OF ASSURANCE

Be assured, children of God,
that God's love for us never ends.
God reaches out to us to forgive our sins,
to heal our brokenness,
and to help us be the loving people we want to be.
Thanks be to God!

QUESTION OF IMPEDIMENT (IF REQUIRED BY LAW OR BY LOCAL CUSTOM)

[To the congregation:]
These two persons have come here
to become one in this holy union.
But if any of you can show just cause why they may not,
declare it now or hereafter remain silent.

[To the couple:]
N. and N., have you come here
freely and without reservation
to join together in this sacred covenant?
[Each responds:]
I have.

DECLARATION OF INTENT

[The presider asks each in turn:]
N., will you take N. to be your *partner/wife/husband*?
Will you share *her/his* joys and burdens?

Will you be honest with *her/him*
and be faithful to *her/him* always,
as long as you both live?
I will.

BLESSING BY THE PARENTS
[To the parents of the couple:]
Will you bless your children in this new relationship?
We will.
May you be blessed with a rich and full life together.

PROMISES AND BLESSINGS BY THE FAMILY
[When children of previous relationships are being brought into the union,
promises and blessings such as the following may be used. The following
forms may be more useful for older children.]

[Each parent says to his/her own children:]
[Name(s) of child(ren),]
I promise that my love and care for you
will continue unchanged, as strong as ever.

[Each of the partners says to the other's children:]
[Name(s) of child(ren),]
I promise to welcome you into my life,
to respect you and honour who you are,
to support [*partner's name*] as your *mother/father*,
to care for you, and allow you to care for me.

[The other's children may respond:]
N., *I/we* **promise to welcome you into** *my/our* **life,**
to respect you and honour who you are,
to support you as *my/our mother's/father's* **partner,**
to care for you and allow you to care for *me/us***.**

[The couple and all the children may say together:]
We make these promises,
trusting not only in our own strength,
but also in the strength of God's love.

PROMISES BY THE COMMUNITY

[To the congregation, who may be invited to stand:]
You have been invited here to witness this covenant:
Will you support N. and N. [and their child(ren)]
with your love, care, and friendship in the years to come?
We will.
[N. and N., we rejoice in your love,
and we will support your marriage today and always.
May God bless you.]

MUSIC

WORD

PRAYER FOR ILLUMINATION

God of us all,
your faithfulness to your covenant
frees us to live together
in the security of your powerful love.
Amid all the changing words of our generation
speak your eternal Word that does not change.
Then may we respond to your gracious promises
by living in faith and obedience;
through our Lord Jesus Christ. **Amen.**

SCRIPTURE

SERMON OR MEDITATION

MUSIC

ACT OF COVENANTING

INVOCATION OF THE SPIRIT

EXCHANGE OF VOWS

[The couple face one another, each holding the right hand of the other. The presider may discreetly help the couple make their vows.]
N., I choose you to be my *partner/wife/husband*,
to laugh with you in joy,

to grieve with you in sorrow,
to grow with you in love,
[to love your child(ren) as you do,]
serving one another and our world in peace and hope,
as long as we both shall live.

EXCHANGE OF RINGS

[If other tokens are used, the presider will make suitable adaptation.]
[The rings may be given to the presider.]
May the circle of these rings
remind you of the love
which encircles you today and always.
May God bless these rings and those who wear them. **Amen.**
[Each places a ring on the other's finger, saying:]
**I give you this ring as a sign of my love
and the vows we have made this day.**

KISS

[The couple may seal their vows with a kiss.]

DECLARATION

N. and N.,
you have committed yourselves to each other
in this joyous and sacred covenant.
May you become one,
fulfilling the promises you have made this day.

BLESSING OF THE COUPLE

N. and N., may God bless you.
May you grow in love,
always delighting in one another,
and remaining faithful to life's end.

May the grace of Christ attend you,
the love of God surround you,
and the Holy Spirit keep you,
now and forever. **Amen.**

PRAYER

[Some or all of the following petitions may be offered.]
Gracious God, we pray for N. and N.
and give thanks that you have brought them together
in this holy union.
Spirit of God,
bless this covenant.

We thank you
for all those whose love has led them
to this day of commitment,
especially for their parents, their friends,
[and their child(ren) N. (and N.),]
those here today and those unable to be here.
Spirit of God,
bless this covenant.

We remember the generations who have gone before us,
[especially . . .]
whom we cannot see, but who are here today in our hearts.
Spirit of God,
bless this covenant.

Help N. and N.
[to be wise and loving parents/family and]
to grow together in faithfulness and honesty,
in mutual support and patience.
Spirit of God,
bless this covenant.

Be with them in their work
and renew them in their leisure,
Spirit of God,
bless this covenant.

Make their life together
a sign of your love in this broken world;
may forgiveness heal injury
and joy overcome sorrow.
Spirit of God,
bless this covenant.

May they welcome into their home
both friends and strangers,
and so reflect Christ's love for all people.
Spirit of God,
bless this covenant.

In all their future together,
may they know joy in each other,
and grow through the love they share.
Spirit of God,
bless this covenant. Amen.

MUSIC

CELEBRATION OF COMMUNION

THE LORD'S PRAYER

SENDING FORTH

MUSIC

SIGNING OF DOCUMENTS
[Documents may be signed at this time or at the end of the service.]

PRESENTATION OF THE COUPLE [AND THEIR CHILDREN]
Will you join me in greeting N. and N.
[and their child(ren) N. (and N.)]
as they begin their new life together.
[The congregation may applaud.]

SENDING FORTH AND BLESSING
Go forth in the love of God;
go forth in hope and joy,
knowing that God is with you.
And the blessing of God,
Creator, Christ, and Spirit,
be with you, and remain with you always. **Amen.**

RECESSIONAL MUSIC

United Church of Christ

Book of Worship

PRELUDE

ENTRANCE

[Banners, ribbons, flowers, candles, white carpeting, or other items may be used in the procession in accordance with local custom. A hymn, psalm, canticle, or anthem may be sung, or instrumental music may be played.]

[The couple to be married may enter the sanctuary together or separately. They may be accompanied by their parents, other members of the family, and friends. People in the congregation who are able may stand for the processional.]

GREETING

[The couple to be married and the wedding party may stand, if they are able, facing the one presiding. The one presiding may use one of the following greetings or another one based on Scripture.]

A

The grace of our Lord Jesus Christ
and the love of God
and the communion of the Holy Spirit
be with you all.
And also with you.

B

Love comes from God.
Everyone who truly loves is a child of God.
Let us worship God.

INTRODUCTION

[The one presiding may state the Christian understanding of marriage, using one of the following or other words.]

A

Dearly beloved, we are gathered here as the people of God
to witness the marriage of N. and N.
We come to share in their joy and to ask God to bless them.

Marriage is a gift of God, sealed by a sacred covenant.
God gives human love.
Through that love, two persons come to know each other
with mutual care and companionship.
God gives joy.
Through that joy, they may share their new life with others
as Jesus shared new wine at the wedding in Cana.
With our love and our prayers,
we support N. and N. as they now freely give themselves to each other.

B

Dear friends, we have come together in the presence of God
to witness the marriage of N. and N.,
to surround them with our prayers,
and to share in their joy.

The Scriptures teach us that the bond and covenant of marriage
is a gift of God,
a holy mystery in which two become one flesh,
an image of the union of Christ and the church.
As this couple give themselves to each other today,
we remember that at Cana in Galilee
our Savior Jesus Christ made the wedding feast
a sign of God's reign of love.
Let us enter into this celebration
confident that through the Holy Spirit,
Christ is present with us now.
We pray that this couple may fulfill God's purpose
for the whole of their lives.

PRAYER

[One of these, a prayer of confession with an assurance of pardon, or a prayer for illumination may be offered.]

Let us pray.

A

O God, we gather to celebrate your gift of love
and its presence among us.
We rejoice that two people have chosen to commit themselves
to a life of loving faithfulness to one another.
We praise you, O God, for the ways you have touched our lives
with a variety of loving relationships.
We give thanks that we have experienced your love
through the life-giving love of Jesus Christ
and through the care and affection of other people.

**At the same time, we remember and confess to you, O God,
that we often have failed to be loving,
that we often have taken for granted the people for whom we
care most.
We selfishly neglect and strain the bonds that unite us with others.
We hurt those who love us
and withdraw from the community that encircles us.
Forgive us, O God.
Renew within us an affectionate spirit.
Enrich our lives with the gracious gift of your love
so that we may embrace others with the same love.
May our participation in this celebration of love and commitment
give to us a new joy and responsiveness to the relationships we
cherish;
through Jesus Christ we pray. Amen.**

Through the great depth and strength of God's love for us,
God reaches out to us to forgive our sins and to restore us to life.
Be assured, children of God,
that God's love enfolds us and upbuilds us
so that we may continue to love one another as God has loved us.

B
Gracious God, always faithful in your love for us,
we rejoice in your presence.
You create love.
You unite us in one human family.
You offer your word and lead us in light.
You open your loving arms and embrace us with strength.
May the presence of Christ fill our hearts with new joy
and make new the lives of your servants whose marriage we
    celebrate.
Bless all creation through this sign of your love
shown in the love of N. and N. for each other.
May the power of your Holy Spirit sustain them and all of us
in love that knows no end. Amen.

READING OF SCRIPTURE

*[The congregation may be seated. One or more Scripture lessons may be
read by the one presiding, by members of the family, or by members of
the wedding party. If Holy Communion is to be celebrated, it is appropriate that the readings include a Gospel lesson. A hymn, a psalm, or other
music may be offered between readings or before or after the sermon.]*

SERMON

*[A brief sermon, charge, or other response to Scripture may be given.
Depending on the religious affiliations of those gathered for the marriage
service, it may be appropriate for all who are able to stand and say a creed
or affirmation of faith.]*

DECLARATION OF INTENTION

[Addressing the couple:]
Before God and this congregation,
I ask you to affirm your willingness to enter this covenant of marriage
and to share all the joys and sorrows of this new relationship,
whatever the future may hold.

[Addressing one:]
N., will you enter into the covenant of marriage with N.,
and will you love *her/him* faithfully as long as you both shall live?
I will, with the help of God.

[Addressing the other:]
N., will you enter into the covenant of marriage with N.,
and will you love *her/him* faithfully as long as you both shall live?
I will, with the help of God.

PLEDGE OF SUPPORT

*[This pledge of support should be used at the discretion of the pastor
and in consultation with the people involved. It allows the family and
congregation to pledge their support and encouragement to the couple. It
is important to consider use of the pledge when there are children from
previous relationships. Children who will share in the new family may
be addressed in these or similar words. They may stand, if able, at their
places or may move near the couple.]*

[Addressing each child by name:]
N.(s), you are entering a new family.
Will you give to this new family your trust, love, and affection?

[Each child responds:]
I will, with the help of God.

[Addressing the couple:]
N. and N., will you be faithful and loving parents to [*names of
child(ren)*]?
We will, with the help of God.

*[The pastor may invite the immediate families of the couple, including
adults or younger children from previous relationships, to stand in place,
if they are able, and to offer their support in these or similar words.]*

[Addressing the families:]
Will the families of N. and N. *please stand/please answer* in support of
this couple. Do you offer your prayerful blessing and loving support to
this marriage? If so, please say, "I do."
I do.

*[All family members may be seated. Anyone who escorted the couple may
be seated with their families. The pastor may address the congregation in
these or similar words.]*

[Addressing the congregation:]
Do you, as people of God,
pledge your support and encouragement to the covenant commitment
that N. and N. are making together?
If so, please say, "We do."
We do.

[An intercessory prayer, using the following or other words, may be offered.]
God of our mothers and of our fathers,
hear our pledges encouraging and supporting this union of N. and N.
Bless us as we offer our prayerful and loving support to their marriage.
Bless them as they pledge their lives to each other.
With faith in you and in each other,
may this couple always bear witness
to the reality of the love to which we witness this day.
May their love continue to grow,
and may it be a true reflection of your love for us all;
through Jesus Christ. **Amen.**

VOWS OF THE MARRIAGE COVENANT
[The pastor may introduce the covenant promises in the following or similar words.]

A
N. and N., by your covenant promises shared with us,
unite yourselves in marriage
and be subject to one another out of reverence for Christ.

B
N. and N., speak your covenant promises
that you have come to offer God.

[If able, the couple may face each other and join hands. Speaking one at a time, they both may say these or other words of covenant.]
N., I give myself to you in the covenant of marriage.
I promise to love and sustain you in this covenant,
from this day forward,
in sickness and in health,
in plenty and in want,

in joy and in sorrow,
as long as we both shall live.

EXCHANGE OF SYMBOLS
[It is recommended that the giving and receiving of rings or other symbols
be shared equally by both partners.]

N. and N., what will you share to symbolize your love?
[The couple may name the symbol(s) and present them/it to the pastor,
who may hold or place a hand on the symbol(s) and offer one of these or
another prayer.]

A
By *these symbols/this symbol* of covenant promise, gracious God,
remind N. and N. of your encircling love and unending faithfulness,
     that in all their life together
they may know joy and peace in one another.
Amen.

B
Eternal God, who in the time of Noah
gave us the rainbow as a sign of promise,
bless *these symbols/this symbol*
that *they/it* also may be *signs/a sign* of promises
fulfilled in lives of faithful loving;
through Jesus Christ our Savior.
Amen.

[If both partners receive symbols, options A and B are used.]

ANNOUNCEMENT OF MARRIAGE
[If able, the couple may stand or kneel and join hands, and the pastor may
place a hand on their joined hands while announcing the marriage, using
one of these or other words.]

A
[Addressing the couple:]
N. and N., you have committed yourselves to each other
in this joyous and sacred covenant.
Become one.
Fulfill your promises.

Love and serve God,
honor Christ and each other,
and rejoice in the power of the Holy Spirit.

[Addressing the congregation:]
By their promises made before us this day,
N. and N. have united themselves in the sacred covenant of marriage.
Those whom God has joined together, let no one separate.

B
[Addressing the congregation:]
Those whom God has joined together let no one separate.

[Addressing the couple:]
N. and N., you are married with the blessing of Christ's church.
Be merciful in all your ways, kind in heart, and humble in mind.
Accept life, and be most patient and tolerant with one another.
Forgive as freely as God has forgiven you.
And, above everything else, be truly loving.
Let the peace of Christ rule in your hearts,
remembering that as members of one body
you are called to live in harmony,
and never forget to be thankful for what God has done for you.

BLESSING
*[If they are able, the couple may stand or kneel, with children who will
share their household, if any, standing nearby. A blessing may be given for
the couple or the family.]*

A, BLESSING FOR THE COUPLE
The grace of Christ attend you;
the love of God surround you;
the Holy Spirit keep you
that you may grow in holy love,
find delight in each other always,
and remain faithful until your life's end.
Amen.

B, BLESSING FOR THE FAMILY

May the God of Sarah and Abraham,
who watches over all the families of the earth,
bless your new family
and establish your home in peace and steadfast love. **Amen.**

PASSING THE PEACE

*[The one presiding may invite those who are able to stand and exchange
gestures of peace.]*
The peace of God be with you always.
And also with you.

*[The couple may embrace. Using the same words as the pastor or similar
ones, they may move among the congregation exchanging the peace. After
passing the peace, the people may be seated, and the couple may return to
their places.]*

[If Holy Communion is to be celebrated, it is to take place here.]

PRAYER OF THANKSGIVING

*[The people may be seated. One of these or a similar prayer of thanksgiv-
ing and intercession may be offered.]*
Let us pray.

A

Most gracious God, we give you thanks for your tender love.
You sent Jesus Christ to come among us,
to be born of a human mother,
and to make the way of the cross into the way of life.
We thank you, too, for consecrating the union of two people in
     Christ's name.

By the power of your Holy Spirit,
pour out the abundance of your blessing on N. and N.
Defend them from every enemy.
Lead them into all peace.
Let their love for each other be a seal on their hearts,
a mantle about their shoulders,
and a crown on their heads.

Bless them in their work and in their companionship,
in their sleeping and in their waking,
in their joys and in their sorrows, in their lives and in their deaths.
Nurture them in a community of the faithful gathered about you.

B
Merciful God, we thank you for your love that lives within us
and calls us from loneliness to companionship.
We thank you for all who have gone before us.
We thank you for our own parents,
and for all, whether married or single,
who are mother or father to us,
and for countless parents whose names we do not know.
We thank you as we grow to the fullness of the stature of Christ.
Bless N. and N.,
that they may have the grace to live the promises they have made.
Defend them from all enemies of their love.
Teach them the patience of undeserved forgiveness.
Bring them to old age,
rejoicing in love's winter more fully than in its springtime.

*[The following words of the prayer may be used if children who will share
in the couple's household are present. If these words are not used, continue
with option A or B of the prayer.]*
Bless *this child/these children*, [*name(s) of children*],
that *he/she/they* may find in this new home
a haven of love and joy
where Jesus Christ is honored in kind words and tender deeds.

A
Finally, in your mercy,
bring N. and N. to that table
where your saints feast forever in your heavenly home;
through Jesus Christ our sovereign Savior who,
with you and the Holy Spirit, lives and reigns,
one God, forever and ever. **Amen.**

B
At the last, receive them and all of us at the love feast
prepared for all the faithful in your eternal home,

where Jesus Christ,
with you and the Holy Spirit,
one God, reigns in love forever. **Amen.**

PRAYER OF OUR SAVIOR

[Standing, sitting, or kneeling, all may sing or say the prayer received from Jesus Christ.]

A

Our Father in heaven, hallowed be your name,
your kingdom come,
your will be done,
on earth as in heaven.
Give us today our daily bread.
Forgive us our sins as we forgive those who sin against us.
Save us from the time of trial and deliver us from evil.
For the kingdom, the power, and the glory are yours
now and forever. Amen.

B

Our Father who art in heaven, hallowed be thy name.
Thy kingdom come.
Thy will be done on earth as it is in heaven.
Give us this day our daily bread.
And forgive us our trespasses,
as we forgive those who trespass against us.
And lead us not into temptation, but deliver us from evil.
For thine is the kingdom, and the power,
and the glory, forever and ever. Amen.

C

Our Father who art in heaven, hallowed be thy name.
Thy kingdom come.
Thy will be done on earth as it is in heaven. Give us this day
our daily bread.
And forgive us our debts, as we forgive our debtors.
And lead us not into temptation, but deliver us from evil.
For thine is the kingdom, and the power,
and the glory, forever. Amen.

D

Our Father-Mother, who is in the heavens,
may your name be made holy,
may your dominion come,
may your will be done,
on the earth as it is in heaven.
Give us today the bread we need;
and forgive us our debts,
as we have forgiven our debtors;
and do not put us to the test,
but rescue us from evil.
For yours is the dominion, and the power, and the glory forever.
    Amen.

[If Holy Communion is not to be celebrated, continue with the benediction.]

ORDER FOR HOLY COMMUNION

[If the sacrament of Holy Communion is to be celebrated, a service of Word and sacrament may be used, beginning with the offering of the Communion elements. The newly married couple, others in the wedding party, or members of the family may bring the Communion elements to the table. The invitation and prayers below may be substituted for ones in a service of Word and sacrament. Holy Communion is properly the supper of Jesus Christ, and all Christians who are present are invited to participate. Practical arrangements for the wedding party will be necessary, such as seats for them during parts of the service.]

INVITATION

[The pastor may go to the table and give this or another invitation.]
This table is open to all who wish to receive Jesus Christ
in company with all believers in all time and beyond time.
This is the joyful feast of the people of God.
Christ is present with gifts of new life,
as once Christ was present at Cana in Galilee with the gift of new wine.
We come to know Christ in the breaking of bread and the pouring of
    wine.

COMMUNION PRAYER

[All who are able may stand. This prayer may replace the Communion prayer in a service of Word and sacrament.]

God be with you.
And also with you.
Lift up your hearts.
We lift them to God.
Let us give thanks to God Most High.
It is right to give God thanks and praise.
Blessed are you, O God our Creator.
From the womb of your being you brought forth worlds.
Into mere dust you blew the breath of life,
creating women and men to bear your likeness in the world.
You create, love, and care for all that is.

We praise and thank you, nurturing God,
that in Jesus you bring joy and hope to loving hearts,
and offer health and power to human relationships.
Even the powers of sorrow and death could not contain Christ's joy.
From the tomb our risen Savior came to share bread again among the
    beloved.
In the glory of your banquet hall,
Christ prepares a wedding feast for all the faithful who even now
    praise you.
Holy. holy, holy God of love and majesty,
the whole universe speaks of your glory, O God Most High.
Blessed is the one who comes in the name of our God!
Hosanna in the highest!

*[The people may be seated or those who are able may kneel. At the words
concerning the bread and wine, the one presiding may indicate the
elements.]*
Merciful God, we remember that on the night of betrayal and desertion,
Jesus took bread, gave thanks to you, broke the bread,
and gave it to the disciples, saying:
"Take and eat, this is my body broken for you."

Likewise, Jesus took the cup of blessing and said:
"Drink of this cup.
It is the new covenant in my blood,
poured out for you and for many for the forgiveness of sins.
Do this in memory of me."

With joy we thank you, God of gladness and warmth,
that at Pentecost you sent your Holy Spirit to dance about the heads
    of your people,
enabling your word to be heard afresh.
Now send your Holy Spirit on these gifts of bread and wine
and on us that we may be set afire with your love and leap with joy
    at your presence.
Pour out your blessing on N. and N.
May they sing a new song of your great love
in communion with you and all your saints in heaven and on earth.
May their love for each other proclaim the love of Christ for all of us.
May the faithful service of all your people
bring peace, justice, joy, and love to all the world;
through Christ, with Christ, and in Christ,
in the unity of the Holy Spirit,
all glory and honor are yours, Holy God, now and forever. **Amen.**

[If the Prayer of Our Savior has not been said earlier in the service, it may be said before the sharing of the Communion elements.]

[The people may come forward or receive the elements where they are seated. If they come forward, the pastor may give each person the bread, and the newly married couple may offer the chalice(s) or individual cups. If trays of individual cups are used, the couple may be positioned at the sides of the pastor, next to attendants with empty trays for the used cups. Hymns of joy and thanksgiving may be sung by the congregation while the elements are being shared.]

PRAYER OF THANKSGIVING
[When all have been served and the table is in order, the wedding party may return to its place and all who are able may stand for the prayer of thanksgiving.]
Let us pray.
Thank you, O God, for refreshing us at your table.
By your grace you have nourished us
with the living presence of Christ, the bread of life,
that we may share life together.
Send us forth in the power of your Holy Spirit
to give ourselves in love
until your entire human family is gathered at your table,
glorifying and praising you in the name of Jesus Christ. Amen.

BENEDICTION

[All who are able may stand. One of these or another blessing may be given for all present.]

A

Go forth in the love of God;
go forth in hope and joy,
knowing that God is with you always.
And the peace of God, which passes all understanding,
keep your hearts and minds
in the knowledge and love of God and of Christ Jesus;
and the blessing of God, Creator, Redeemer, and Sanctifier,
be with you, and remain with you always. **Amen.**

B

May God bless you and keep you.
May God's face shine upon you and be gracious to you.
May God look upon you with kindness and give you peace. **Amen.**

HYMN OR POSTLUDE

[A hymn may be sung or other suitable music offered as the wedding party and congregation depart.]

Presbyterian Church (U.S.A.)

Adapted from *The Book of Common Worship*, Rite I

ENTRANCE

[As the people gather, music appropriate to the praise of God may be offered. At the appointed time, the couple and other members of the wedding party enter and stand before the minister. Family members may stand with the couple.]

[During the entrance of the wedding party, the people may stand and sing a psalm, hymn, or spiritual. Or an anthem may be sung, or instrumental music played.]

SENTENCES OF SCRIPTURE

[The minister calls the people to worship, either before or after the entrance, using one of the following, or another appropriate verse from Scripture.]

A

God is love,
and those who abide in love
abide in God,
and God abides in them.

1 John 4:16

B

This is the day that the Lord has made;
let us rejoice and be glad in it.

Ps. 118:24

C

O give thanks, for the Lord is good.
God's love endures forever.

Ps. 106:1

STATEMENT ON THE GIFT OF MARRIAGE

We gather in the presence of God
to give thanks for the gift of marriage,
to witness the joining together of N. and N.,
to surround them with our prayers,
and to ask God's blessing upon them,
so that they may be strengthened for their life together
and nurtured in their love for God.

God created us,
and gave us marriage
so that two people may help and comfort each other,
living faithfully together in plenty and in want,
in joy and in sorrow,
in sickness and in health,
throughout all their days.

God gave us marriage
for the full expression of the love between two people.
In marriage they belong to each other,
and with affection and tenderness
freely give themselves to each other.

God gave us marriage
for the well-being of human society,
for the ordering of family life,
and for the birth and nurture of children.

God gave us marriage as a holy mystery
in which two people are joined together,
and become one,
just as Christ is one with the church.

In marriage, they are called to a new way of life,
created, ordered, and blessed by God.
This way of life must not be entered into carelessly,
or from selfish motives,
but responsibly, and prayerfully.

We rejoice that marriage is given by God,
blessed by our Lord Jesus Christ,
and sustained by the Holy Spirit.
Therefore, let marriage be held in honor by all.

PRAYER

Let us pray:

Gracious God,
you are always faithful in your love for us.
Look mercifully upon N. and N.,
who have come seeking your blessing.
Let your Holy Spirit rest upon them
so that with steadfast love
they may honor the promises they make this day,
through Jesus Christ our Savior. **Amen.**
[The congregation may be seated.]

DECLARATIONS OF INTENT

*[The minister addresses members of the couple individually, using either
A or B:]*

A

N., understanding that God has created, ordered, and blessed the
covenant of marriage,
do you affirm your desire and intention to enter this covenant?
I do.

B

[If both are baptized, the following may be used:]
N., in your baptism
you have been called to union with Christ and the church.
Do you intend to honor this calling
through the covenant of marriage?
I do.

AFFIRMATIONS OF THE FAMILIES

[The minister may address the families of the couple:]
[Names of family members],
do you give your blessing to N. and N.,

and promise to do everything in your power to uphold them
in their marriage?
[The families of the couple answer:]

A

**We (I) give our (my) blessing
and promise our (my) loving support.**

B

We (I) do.

[The families of the couple may be seated.]

AFFIRMATION OF THE CONGREGATION
[The minister may address the congregation, saying:]
Will all of you witnessing these vows
do everything in your power
to uphold N. and N. in their marriage?
We will.

[A psalm, hymn, spiritual, or anthem may be sung.]

READING FROM SCRIPTURE
God of mercy,
your faithfulness to your covenant
frees us to live together
in the security of your powerful love.
Amid all the changing words of our generation,
speak your eternal Word that does not change.
Then may we respond to your gracious promises
by living in faith and obedience;
through our Lord Jesus Christ.
Amen.

[One or more Scripture passages are read.]

SERMON
[After the Scriptures are read, a brief sermon may be given.]

[A psalm, hymn, spiritual, or other music may follow.]

VOWS

[The people may stand.]
[The minister addresses the couple:]
N. and N.,
since it is your intention to marry,
join your right hands,
and with your promises
bind yourselves to each other in the covenant of marriage.

A

I, N., take you, N., to be my beloved;
and I promise,
before God and these witnesses,
to be loving and faithful
in plenty and in want;
in joy and in sorrow;
in sickness and in health;
as long as we both shall live.

B

Before God and these witnesses,
I, N., take you, N., to be my own,
and I promise to love you,
and to be faithful to you,
as long as we both shall live.

EXCHANGE OF RINGS (OR OTHER SYMBOLS)

[If rings are to be exchanged, the minister may say to the couple:]
What do you bring as the sign of your promise?

[When the rings are presented, the minister may say the following prayer.]
By your blessing, O God,
may these rings be to N. and N.
symbols of unending love and faithfulness,
reminding them of the covenant they have made this day,
through Jesus Christ our Lord. **Amen.**

[Rings are exchanged using A or B or other appropriate words. The traditional Trinitarian formula should be omitted if one of the marriage partners is not a professing Christian.]

A

[The one giving the ring says:]

N., I give you this ring as a sign of our covenant,
in the name of the Father,
and of the Son,
and of the Holy Spirit.

[The one receiving the ring says:]

I receive this ring as a sign of our covenant,
in the name of the Father,
and of the Son,
and of the Holy Spirit.

B

[As each ring is given, the one giving the ring says:]

This ring I give you,
as a sign of our constant faith
and abiding love,
in the name of the Father,
and of the Son,
and of the Holy Spirit.

PRAYER

[The couple may kneel.]
[One of the following prayers, or a similar prayer, is said:]
Let us pray:

A

Eternal God,
Creator and preserver of all life,
author of salvation, and giver of all grace:
look with favor upon the world you have made and redeemed,
and especially upon N. and N.

Give them wisdom and devotion
in their common life,
that each may be to the other
a strength in need,
a counselor in perplexity,
a comfort in sorrow,
and a companion in joy.

Grant that their wills
may be so knit together in your will,
and their spirits in your Spirit,
that they may grow in love and peace
with you and each other
all the days of their life.

Give them the grace,
when they hurt each other,
to recognize and confess their fault,
and to seek each other's forgiveness
and yours.

Make their life together
a sign of Christ's love
to this sinful and broken world,
that unity may overcome estrangement,
forgiveness heal guilt,
and joy conquer despair.

Give them such fulfillment of their mutual love
that they may reach out in concern for others.

[Give to them, if it is your will,
the gift of children,
and the wisdom to bring them up
to know you,
to love you,
and to serve you.]

Grant that all who have witnessed these vows today
may find their lives strengthened,
and that all who are married
may depart with their own promises renewed.

Enrich us all with your grace
that, loving and supporting one another,
we may serve those in need
and be a sign of your kingdom.

Grant that the bonds by which all your children
are united to one another
may be so transformed by your Spirit
that your peace and justice may fill the earth,
through Jesus Christ our Lord. **Amen.**

B
Eternal God,
without your grace no promise is sure.
Strengthen N. and N.
with patience, kindness, gentleness,
and all other gifts of your Spirit,
so that they may fulfill the vows they have made.
Keep them faithful to each other and to you.
Fill them with such love and joy
that they may build a home of peace and welcome.
Guide them by your Word
to serve you all their days.

Help us all, O God,
to do your will in each of our homes and lives.
Enrich us with your grace
so that, supporting one another,
we may serve those in need
and hasten the coming of peace, love, and justice on earth,
through Jesus Christ our Lord. **Amen.**

LORD'S PRAYER

[The minister invites all present to sing or say the Lord's Prayer.]
As our Savior Christ has taught us, we are bold to say:
Our Father in heaven,
hallowed be your name,
your kingdom come,
your will be done,
on earth as in heaven.
Give us today our daily bread.
Forgive us our sins
as we forgive those who sin against us.
Save us from the time of trial
and deliver us from evil.

For the kingdom, the power,
and the glory are yours
now and forever. Amen.

ANNOUNCEMENT OF MARRIAGE
[The minister addresses the congregation:]
Before God and in the presence of this congregation,
N. and N. have made their solemn vows to each other.
They have confirmed their promises by the joining of hands
[and by the giving and receiving of rings].
Therefore, I proclaim that they are now married.
Blessed be the Father and the Son and the Holy Spirit now and forever.
[The minister joins the couple's right hands.]
[The congregation may join the minister in saying:]
**Those whom God has joined together
let no one separate.**

CHARGE AND BLESSING

CHARGE TO THE COUPLE
[The minister addresses the couple, using one of the following:]

A
As God's own,   *Col. 3:12–14*
clothe yourselves with compassion,
kindness, and patience,
forgiving each other
as the Lord has forgiven you,
and crown all these things with love,
which binds everything together in perfect harmony.

B
Whatever you do, in word or deed,   *Col. 3:17*
do everything in the name of the Lord Jesus,
giving thanks to God through him.

BLESSING
*[The minister gives God's blessing to the couple and the congregation,
using one of the following:]*

A

The Lord bless you and keep you.

The Lord be kind and gracious to you.

The Lord look upon you with favor

and give you peace. **Amen.**

Num. 6:24–26

B

The grace of Christ attend you,

the love of God surround you,

the Holy Spirit keep you,

that you may live in faith,

abound in hope,

and grow in love,

both now and forevermore. **Amen.**

[A psalm, hymn, spiritual, or anthem may be sung, or instrumental music may be played, as the wedding party leaves.]

Reaffirmation of Vows A

[This service might be used for couples previously married in a civil ceremony who wish to reaffirm their vows in the context of a service of Christian worship. This brief rite would appropriately follow the proclamation of the Word.]

OPENING SENTENCES

Make a joyful noise to the Lord, all the earth.   *Ps. 100:1–2, 4–5*
Worship the Lord with gladness;
come into God's presence with singing.
Enter God's gates with thanksgiving.
Give thanks to God,
blessing God's name.
For the Lord is good;
God's steadfast love endures forever,
with faithfulness to all generations.

OPENING STATEMENT

Dear people of God,
we have gathered to worship God
and to remember and celebrate
promises made and promises kept.
We remember that God first loved us
and has been steadfast and faithful to us
throughout all our years.
As seasons change,
and year follows year,
the sure presence of God
remains constant.
In this is our hope—

not that we have loved God,   *1 John 4:10–11*
but that God first loved us.
God calls us to love one another.

Today we celebrate that ___ years ago,
N. and N. came before God
to make promises to each other,
a commitment to live and love together.
Now they invite us,
as family members and friends,
to surround them once again
with love and support
as they reaffirm their love
and their intention
to live in faithfulness with God
and with each other.

PRAYER

Holy and gracious God,
you surround and uphold us
in every moment of life.
You gift us with family and friends for the journey,
making our lives more abundant
than they might otherwise have been.
We give thanks for such enduring relationships.

We thank you especially
for the love and faithfulness N. and N. share.
As they reaffirm promises made long ago,
give fresh grace to them
for the years ahead.
By the power of your Holy Spirit,
bless their memories
and strengthen their hopes
so their joy may be full.
In Jesus Christ we pray. **Amen.**

SCRIPTURE READINGS

Hebrews 11:1–3, 8–10, 13–16
2 Corinthians 5:16–20

SERMON/HOMILY

[In this service, as the Scripture readings and liturgy suggest, the theme of journey is prominent. In a service where vows are reaffirmed and renewed, there is a past to remember and to celebrate and a future journey still unfolding. A homily on this theme might remember how God journeyed with Israel through the centuries in times of plenty and want, sickness and health, exile and homecoming. Jesus, too, journeyed with his disciples, and the church has journeyed with the Spirit of God through many surprising and changing circumstances of reformation and renewal. The faithfulness of God along the way of life provides a template for the faithfulness and grace we are to share in our journey together. Along the way, it is good and right to pause and consider all that has been and to recommit ourselves for all that is to come in our most intimate of relationships. It may also be appropriate, as this service suggests, for the service to recall the larger community of faith in which God places us and our service together in God's name.]

REAFFIRMATION OF VOWS

[Each says to the other:]

N., ___ years ago,
I stood before God
and pledged my love to you.
I reaffirm my vow
to love and honor you,
giving thanks for what has been
and looking forward to all that will be.
I will continue to share the journey of life with you
in faith and hope,
with God's help.

[If new symbols or rings are to be exchanged:]

PRAYER OF BLESSING

Loving God,
we are encircled by your eternal love.
Today N. and N. are encircled
in the love of family and friends
as they reaffirm their vows.
We ask your blessing upon
these symbols of reaffirmation.

Whenever N. and N.
look upon these signs of unending love and faithfulness,
let them remember this day with thanksgiving
and so be renewed
in mind and heart and spirit.
Through Jesus Christ our Lord. **Amen.**

SYMBOLS/RINGS GIVEN AND RECEIVED
[Each says to the other as the symbol or ring is given:]
N., I give you this sign of our love,
reaffirmed this day,
in tender hope for what lies ahead;
in the name of God
whose steadfast love endures forever.

PRAYER OF BLESSING
Holy and wondrous God,
as you accompanied our ancestors,
so you journey with us to our life's end;
you will offer life abundant
in your eternal realm.
We give thanks today
that we stand in company of the faithful,
grateful recipients
of your steadfast faithfulness and love.

We pray your continued blessing
upon N. and N.
in their life together.
May they continue to grow in mutual love,
extend forgiveness when they hurt each other,
practice patience in adversity,
set a table of hospitality,
and be lifted in joy,
all in service to your kingdom.

Grant that we,
who have witnessed their reaffirmation of vows,
may find our own promises renewed
and our faith strengthened
so that, in joy and love,

we may continue the journey set before us
with courage and hope.
May our own lives bear witness
to the grace we have received from you,
God of the past,
the present,
and the future.
In Christ's name we pray. **Amen.**

CHARGE

Hear the words of Paul to the gathered faithful in Philippi:
Finally, beloved,   *Phil. 4:8–9*
whatever is true,
whatever is honorable,
whatever is just,
whatever is pure,
whatever is pleasing,
whatever is commendable,
if there is any excellence
and if there is anything worthy of praise,
think about these things.
Keep on doing the things
you have learned and received
and heard and seen in me,
and the God of peace will be with you.

BENEDICTION

In wilderness and promised land,
God be with you;
on the way of discipleship,
the grace of Christ attend you;
and for all that is to come,
the joy of the Spirit guide you,
today and all your days.

Reaffirmation of Marriage Vows B

[This service might be used for couples previously married in a civil ceremony who wish to reaffirm their vows in the context of a service of Christian worship. This brief rite would appropriately follow the proclamation of the Word*]

SENTENCES OF SCRIPTURE

God is love, *1 John 4:16*
and those who abide in love
abide in God,
and God abides in them.

THE GIFT OF MARRIAGE

Today we celebrate the abiding love of N. and N.,
who were married ___ years ago on [date].
On that day they spoke vows pledging their loyalty and love.
Now, in the presence of God and the church,
they come to reaffirm those vows
and in faith to confess their common purpose in the Lord.

We gather to give thanks to God for the gift of marriage,
to witness their promises to each other,
to surround them with our prayers,
and to ask God's blessing upon them,
so that they may be strengthened for their life together
and nurtured in their love for God.

---

*Adapted from Christian Marriage Rite III in the Presbyterian *Book of Common Worship* (Louisville, KY: Westminster/John Knox Press, 1993), 882–92.

We rejoice that marriage is given by God,
   blessed by our Lord Jesus Christ,
   and sustained by the Holy Spirit.
Therefore, let marriage be held in honor by all.

REAFFIRMATION OF VOWS
[The couple join hands. Each says:]
N., you are my beloved,
and I promise,
before God and these witnesses,
to be loving and faithful;
in plenty and in want;
in joy and in sorrow;
in sickness and in health;
as long as we both shall live.

PRAYER
Eternal God,
without your grace no promise is sure.
Strengthen N. and N. with patience, kindness, gentleness,
and all other gifts of your Spirit,
so that they may continue to fulfill the vows they have made.
Keep them faithful to each other and to you.
Fill them with such love and joy
that they may build a home of peace and welcome.
Guide them by your Word
to serve you all their days.
Help us all, O God,
to do your will in each of our homes and lives.
Enrich us with your grace
so that, supporting one another,
we may serve those in need
and hasten the coming of peace, love, and justice on earth,
through Jesus Christ our Lord. **Amen.**

CHARGE
As God's own, *Col. 3:12–14*
clothe yourselves with compassion,
kindness, and patience,

forgiving each other
as the Lord has forgiven you,
and crown all these things with love,
which binds everything together
in perfect harmony.

BLESSING

The grace of Christ attend you,
the love of God surround you,
the Holy Spirit keep you,
that you may live in faith,
abound in hope,
and grow in love,
both now and forevermore. **Amen.**

PART 2

❧ **SOURCEBOOK** ☙

Additional Liturgical Material

Hymns

Prayers for Particular Occasions

❧ *Additional Liturgical Material* ❦

This material contains additional options for each part
of the service followed by the options provided in the
full liturgies. New material is presented first in each section.

Greeting

A

The grace and peace
of the Lord be with you.
And also with you.

B

The grace of Christ be with you.
And also with you.
The love of God be with you.
And also with you.

C

The life of the Spirit be with you.
And also with you.
Let us worship God.

D

The God of faith, hope, and love
be with you all.
And also with you.

E

N. and N.,
the Lord be with you.
And also with you.
People of God,
the Lord be with you.
And also with you.
Let us worship God.

Opening Sentences

[One or more of the following may be said.]

A

How precious is your steadfast love, O God! *Ps. 36:7*
All people find shelter in the shadow of your wings.

B

Steadfast love and faithfulness will meet; *Ps. 85:10*
righteousness and peace will kiss.

C

This is the day the Lord has made! *Ps. 118:24*
Let us rejoice and be glad in it.

D

How very good and pleasant it is *Ps. 133*
when kindred live together in unity!
It is like precious oil on the head,
running down the beard of Aaron,
running down over the collar of his robes.
It is like the dew of Hermon,
which falls on the mountains of Zion.
For there the Lord ordained blessing,
life forevermore.

E

The steadfast love of the Lord never ceases;   *Lam. 3:22–23*
God's mercies never come to an end.
The grace of God is new every morning;
great is the faithfulness of the Lord.

F

Give thanks to the Lord, for God is good;   *1 Chr. 16:34*
God's steadfast love endures forever.

G

The Lord is God, the Lord alone.   *Mark 12:29–31*
Let us love the Lord our God
with all our heart
and with all our soul
and with all our mind
and with all our strength.
And let us love our neighbors
as ourselves.

H

Jesus said: I give you a new commandment,   *John 13:34–35*
that you love one another.
Just as I have loved you,
you also should love one another.
By this everyone will know
that we are disciples of Jesus Christ,
if we have love for one another.

I

As many of you as were baptized into Christ   *Gal. 3:27–28*
have clothed yourselves with Christ.
There is no longer Jew or Greek,
there is no longer slave or free,
there is no longer male and female;
for all of you are one in Christ Jesus.

J

Now, beloved, put on the garment of love,   *Col. 3:14*
for love binds all things together in harmony.

K

Let us love one another, for love is from God. *1 John 4:7*
All those who have love are children of God.

L

God's love was revealed among us
when God sent the only Son into the world
so that we might live through him. *1 John 4:9*

M

God is love,
and those who abide in love abide in God,
and God abides in them. *1 John 4:16b*

N

God is love, *1 John 4:16–19*
and those who abide in love
abide in God.
There is no fear in love,
but perfect love casts out fear.
We love because God first loved us.

Call to Worship

A
Where love is given and received,
God is with us.
Where love is shared in word and action,
God is with us.
Where love is known in lives made new,
God is with us.
Where love is held in honor by all,
God is with us.
Let us worship God.

B
The time has come   *Ps. 85:10–11*
for steadfast love and faith to meet,
for righteousness and peace to kiss,
for earth and heaven to rejoice.
Let us worship God.

C
Many roads have converged in this place.
Many paths have brought us to this day.
The God of grace has called us here.
The God of peace surrounds us now.
N., and N., now you will journey on together.
You will go forward, hand in hand.
Where love is known in word and deed,
God is with us.

Where love is shared with all in need,
God is with us.
Let us worship God.

D
[Water is poured into the font.]
Many waters cannot quench love.
In the gracious waters of baptism,
God has claimed us as God's own beloved children
and promised to be our God for all eternity.
As N. and N. make their promises to each other in the covenant
of marriage,
they respond to God's prior promise to them in baptism
and in the strength of God's steadfast love.

E
Today we gather
in the presence of God
to witness the joy
of two lives becoming one.
Let us worship God.

F
Beloved people,
in the name of God
I welcome you
to the marriage of N. and N.
Let us worship God.

G
This is the day our God has made.
Let us rejoice and be glad in it.

May the faithfulness of God,
the presence of Christ,
and the life of the Holy Spirit
be with you all.
And also with you.

H

We gather to worship God,
whose love is abounding and steadfast,   *Exod. 34:6*
whose faithfulness never comes to an end.
As the family and friends of N. and N.,
we gather to witness their vows to one another,
celebrate the promises they make this day,
and surround them with our prayers,
that their love may grow
and all creation may flourish with new life.

Statement on Marriage

[Wedding services often begin with a brief statement that affirms biblical and theological understandings of marriage. Such a statement calls attention to the gifts of God given in marriage, identifies marriage as a calling, and names the importance of the gathered community who upholds the couple with prayer.]

A

What is marriage?
Marriage is a gift of God for all people,
and a human institution, for the sake of social order.
For Christians, marriage is a covenant relationship,
a new way of life together, in Jesus' name.

With thanks and praise to God, we gather here
to witness the marriage of N. and N.,
and to pray for God's blessing in their lives.
God created us and calls us into relationship
to love and care for one another.
Through God's gift of marriage
we show affection, practice generosity,
create new homes and new families,
and become one body, like the church.

Marriage is a gift and a calling—
a deep commitment, a holy covenant,
a new way of life in Jesus' name.
Thanks be to God for this gift of marriage,
and for the marriage of N. and N.
that we celebrate this day.

B

Beloved, love is from God.

Everyone who loves is born of God and knows God.

At the beginning of time, God said that it was not good to be alone
and created us to be in relationship with others.

Made in the image of God,
we are given the capacity to love and be loved.

The making of promises is a sacramental sign
of God's faithfulness and intention for the whole creation.

God blesses those who love one another
and promises to be an ever-present source of strength
for those who build a life together.

On this day, we gather as a community of friends
to witness this new step in N. and N.'s journey.

We recognize that the support of community is essential,
and we give thanks that we can offer our prayers,
our solidarity, and our friendship
to N. and N. for their life together.

C

Beloved Community,

God has created us to be in relationship with the Divine,
with other people,
and with all creation.

Christian marriage is a visible sign
of unity in a broken world
and a covenant call to faithfulness.

In Christian marriage,
two people commit to a way of life together
that is marked by love, joy, peace,   *Gal. 5:22–23*
patience, kindness, generosity, and self-control—
gifts of the Holy Spirit
available to all.

Marriage can be a haven from the storms of life,
a place of refuge and lodging;
and it is also an invitation
to reach out in wide and generous welcome
to stranger, and neighbor, and friend.

Into this estate,
N. and N. come now to be joined.

D

We gather here, in God's presence,
to witness the marriage of N. and N.,
surrounding them with our joy,
embracing them with our support,
and upholding them in our prayers.
Marriage is a gift from God—
the gift of love between two people
who promise to care for one another
and be faithful in the love they share.
Marriage is a new way of life—
the joining together of two people
who promise to seek the common good
and reach out with love to others.

E

Sisters and brothers,
we are gathered here to celebrate the union of N. and N.,
to witness the vows they make to one another,
to pledge our support and encouragement,
and to seek God's blessing upon their marriage.

God created us for companionship
and gave us the capacity for joy.
Jesus Christ showed us self-giving love
and taught us to continually forgive.
And the Holy Spirit, given in our baptism,
renews grace within us day by day
and enables us to grow in faith, in hope, and in love.

Marriage is a gift and a calling
in which two people become for one another
a source of love,
a fount of blessing,
and a deep well of grace,
bearing each other's burdens
and sharing in each other's joys.

As N. and N. commit their lives to one another,
families are joined,
friendships are forged and strengthened,
and a new community of love is formed.

As we bear witness to the vows being made today,
let us surround N. and N. with affection and prayer,
giving thanks for all the ways
that God's love is made manifest in our lives.

F
We have come together in the presence of God,
for the marriage of N. and N.;
to share their joy, and to promise them our support and love.

Marriage is a gift of God
and a means of grace.
In the lifelong union of marriage
we can know the joy of God,
who made us in his own image.

Marriage is founded in God's loving nature,
and in God's covenant of love with us in Christ.
Two people,
in giving themselves to each other in love,
reflect the love of Christ for his church.

When Christians marry
they are called
to live faithfully together,
to love each other with respect,
tenderness, and delight.

They share the life of a home
[and may be trusted
with the gift and care of children].
They help to shape a society
in which human dignity and happiness
may flourish and abound.

Our Lord Jesus Christ was himself
a guest at a wedding in Cana of Galilee.
Through his Spirit he is with us now,
to enrich our love
and to give us his peace and joy.

G

Marriage is a gift of God
and a means of grace.
In the lifelong union of marriage
we can know the joy of God,
in whose image we are made.

Marriage is founded in God's loving nature,
and in the covenant of love made with us in Christ.
Two partners,
in giving themselves to each other in love,
reflect the love of Christ for his church.

In Christian marriage,
each person is called
to live together faithfully,
and to love the other with respect,
tenderness, and delight.
The companionship and comfort of marriage
enables the full expression
of physical love between the two partners.

They share the life of a home
[and may be entrusted
with the gift and care of children].
They help to shape a society
in which human dignity and happiness
may flourish and abound.

Marriage is a way of life that all people should honour;
it is not to be entered into lightly or selfishly,
but responsibly and in the love of God.

N. and N. are now to begin this way of life
that God has created and Christ has blessed.
Therefore, on this their wedding day,
we pray that they may fulfil God's purpose
for the whole of their lives.

Prayer of the Day

[A prayer offered at the beginning of a wedding service acknowledges the love of God as the basis of all love, asks for God's blessing during the wedding and beyond, and affirms our hope in God's future.]

A

[At the baptismal font:]
Lord God, from whom all blessings flow,
your Word is the source of our faith;
your Spirit is the source of our hope;
your love is the source of our love.
Pour out your blessing upon N. and N.,
that by the gift of your Word and Spirit
they may come to know the holy mystery
of deep and abiding communion with you.
Encircle and embrace them this day,
so that, by your grace, they may truly be
one in faith, one in hope, one in love;
one in you, now and forever. **Amen.**

B

God of love,
we belong to you
and to one another.
Bind us,
hearts and hands,
to the whole communion of saints this day,
so that your love,

its breadth and length and height and depth, *Eph. 3:18*
fills all in all,
making us one family
in heaven and on earth.
In Christ's name, we pray. **Amen.**

C
God of life and love,
thank you for leading N. and N. to one another,
for planting in them the seeds of mutual love,
and bringing them to this day of promise making.

We love because you first loved us;
we dare to make vows because
you have made a covenant with us.
In Jesus Christ, you showed us how to give of ourselves to others
and taught us how to forgive.

Shine your light on us today,
and especially upon N. and N.,
as they bind themselves to one another.
By your Spirit may they know the promise of your deep and
    abiding love
this day, and through all the days to come.
In Jesus' name we pray. **Amen.**

D
God of wonder and delight,
when you crafted human beings with your own hands
and breathed into them the breath of life,
you set into motion a love that would shape all of history.
Breathe that same spirit into this marriage between N. and N.
You have provided for them since the beginning;
now give them courage to make their promises,
and the creativity to keep them,
until that day when you gather us all into the celebration
that will have no end.
In Jesus' name we pray. **Amen.**

E

Gracious God, your glory shines.   *Isa. 60:1, 5*
We see your radiance,
and our hearts rejoice.
You have given us gift upon gift
until we are filled with gratitude.
Now we thank you for the way love comes to us,
like grace,
immeasurable, unearned.
Especially we thank you for the love
that N. and N. have come to profess.
Bless the promises they will make this day.
Strengthen them in their life together.
Be to us all an everlasting light   *Isa. 60:19c, 21b*
and make us the work of your own hands—
all for your glory.
In Christ's name, we pray. **Amen.**

F

Gracious God,
we thank you for all the gifts of your love,
and especially for the gift of marriage.

We praise you for your guidance
in the lives of N. and N.,
for the joy they find in each other,
and for the love and trust they bring
to the happiness of this day.

And since we know that without you
nothing is strong, nothing is holy,
we pray that you will enrich them
with your grace
as they make their marriage covenant together.
Grant that your joy may be in them,
and that their joy may be full;
through Jesus Christ our Lord. **Amen.**

Prayer of Confession and
Declaration of Forgiveness

[All people—even those who love each other deeply—hurt each other and fail to live as God intends. Confessing sin, and hearing words of forgiveness, allows grace to be spoken at a wedding. All who are present hear of God's mercy, and couples make their vows as forgiven people who seek to forgive one another. The selections below each contain a Call to Confession, a Prayer of Confession, and a Declaration of Forgiveness. It is intended that these three elements be used together.]

A

CALL TO CONFESSION

On this day of deep joy and bright hope,
let us confess before God and one another
our need for grace.
Even as we make promises to one another,
we acknowledge our capacity to do harm,
that we may receive pardon from our God,
who waits in mercy to forgive.

PRAYER OF CONFESSION

Gracious God,
we confess that we do not always keep faith
with you or one another.
We tear down when we should build up;
we hurt one another when we mean to be kind;
we fail to forgive as you have forgiven us.

Have mercy on us, O God.
Soften our hearts,
enlarge our capacity to care,
and conform our wills to your own,
that we may love one another well
and serve you with joy.
In Jesus' name we pray. Amen.

DECLARATION OF FORGIVENESS
Hear the good news!
[Water may be poured into the baptismal font.]
In the waters of baptism we are given new life,
freed from the sin that binds us,
and sent forth to reflect the light of Christ
to all we meet.

Sisters and brothers, believe the gospel!
In Jesus Christ, we are forgiven.
Thanks be to God!

B

CALL TO CONFESSION
[From the baptismal font, the minister says:]
Thus says the Lord, who created you: *Isa. 43:1–2*
Do not fear, for I have redeemed you;
I have called you by name, you are mine.
When you pass through the waters,
I will be with you;
when you walk through the fire
you will not be burned.

Trusting in God's steadfast love,
let us confess our sin.

PRAYER OF CONFESSION
**God of overflowing grace,
we confess that we have failed
to live according to your way
of faithfulness and steadfast love.**

You call us to live in faith
but we continue to live in fear.
You set us free from the power of evil
but we are still captivated by sin.
You lead us into a new way of life
but we remain in the ways of death.

Forgive us, loving God.
Open our hearts to the gift of your grace,
transform our lives by your Holy Spirit,
and teach us to love one another,
even as you have loved us;
through Jesus Christ our Savior.

DECLARATION OF FORGIVENESS

Hear God's word of grace for you: *Isa. 43:4, 18–19*
You are precious in my sight,
and honored, and I love you.

[Lifting water from the font:]
Do not remember the former things.
I am doing a new thing;
now it springs forth—do you see it?

Friends, believe the good news:

In Jesus Christ, we are forgiven.
Thanks be to God.

C

CALL TO CONFESSION

On this day of promise making
we acknowledge that we often fail
to live up to our good intentions
and fall short of living the life God wants for us.
Yet God, whose faithfulness never ends,
waits in mercy to forgive.
Together, let us confess our sin before God and one another.

PRAYER OF CONFESSION

 God of mercy,
 you know the ways we have broken covenant with you,
 and those we love,
 those present and those absent this day,
 and with others, too, along the way.
 You know the brokenness multiplied in the world:
 our conflicts unresolved;
 our prejudices unrelenting;
 and our injustices unrestrained.

 Forgive us, we pray,
 for the wrong we have done
 and the hurt we have inflicted.
 Increase our capacity to love,
 to forgive,
 and to seek peace
 in our families,
 in the church,
 and in the world.
 We pray in the name of Christ,
 who has come to tear down our dividing walls. Amen. *Eph. 2:14*

DECLARATION OF FORGIVENESS

 Hear the good news!
 In Christ we have been cleansed from our sin
 and set free from all that binds us.
 Anyone who is in Christ is a new creation!
 The old life is gone and a new life has begun.
 In Jesus Christ, we are forgiven.

D

CALL TO CONFESSION

 God desires that all creation might be one;
 that love be central to human life;
 and that all may know peace and mercy.
 Trusting in God's mercy,
 let us come before God to confess that sin has often
 broken our relationships and brought pain to the creation.

PRAYER OF CONFESSION

Gracious God,
we have not always followed your command
to fill the earth with blessing.
We have hurt the people we love the most;
we have shown little concern for those we do not know.
Our society has created barriers and sent minorities to the margins.
Our church has not offered its blessing as Christ commanded us.

Forgive us, and give us strength to right the wrongs of the past.
Open our hearts to your ever-widening love,
and make us advocates for justice.
Bind our hearts to the forgiveness that you offer,
and let us never tire of practicing mercy.
In Jesus' name we pray. Amen.

DECLARATION OF FORGIVENESS

God never turns from us,
but works within the creation to bring us home.
The forgiveness that God offers in Jesus Christ is yours.
Heaven rejoices when all are gathered into joyful celebration.
Enter this joy, and be at peace,
now and forever.
Amen.

E

CALL TO CONFESSION

The God of grace,
who knows our inmost thoughts
and sees our failings,
waits in mercy to forgive.
In faith, let us confess our sin
before God and one another.

PRAYER OF CONFESSION

Merciful God,
we fail to live by your Word
and do not keep faith with you or one another.

Take the promises
that lie broken on the floors of our lives;
sweep them away,
or make of the shards a new design.
Turn us back to you
until good intentions
become deeds of justice and love.
To turn will be our delight,
for in turning,
we return
to you and to one another,
a new creation in Jesus Christ,   *2 Cor. 5:17*
through whom we pray. Amen.

DECLARATION OF FORGIVENESS
Friends,
forgiveness comes from God,   *2 Cor. 5:19–20*
who is not counting our trespasses against us.
For God has reconciled us through Christ,
and entrusts to us the message of reconciliation.
We are ambassadors for Christ,
sharing his peace with all.
The peace of the Lord Jesus Christ be with you.
And also with you.

[The people may exchange signs of peace with one another.]

F

CALL TO CONFESSION
Love is not always easy.
Loving one another requires patience, faith, strength, and hope.
Often we make mistakes,
failing to live up to our visions and God's hopes.
Let us come before God in confession,

PRAYER OF CONFESSION
God of love,
in the warmth of your presence,

and in the warmth of the love celebrated here today,
we confess our failures to love.
We love ourselves,
but not enough to honour your image in us.
We love others,
but not enough to always be patient, gentle, and kind.
Forgive us.
Lead us in your way
that we may truly and rightly love you,
ourselves, and others. Amen.

DECLARATION OF FORGIVENESS
Be assured, children of God,
that God's love for us never ends.
God reaches out to us to forgive our sins,
to heal our brokenness,
and to help us be the loving people we want to be.
Thanks be to God!

Declaration of Intent

A
Marriage is a holy bond
of steadfast love and faithfulness
between two people.
N., do you desire to join N.
in the covenant of marriage?
I do.

B
[When the marriage takes place at the font:]
As Christ shares his life with the church
through the covenant of baptism,
N., do you wish to share your life with N.
in the covenant of marriage?
I do.

C
[When the Eucharist is included:]
As Jesus freely gives himself to us
at the table he prepares,
N., do you freely give yourself to N.
in the covenant of marriage?
I do.

D
N., do you freely choose N.
and intend to enter the covenant of marriage?
I do.

E

N., you have shared your life with N. for these last ___ years.
Do you intend to continue in this relationship,
to mature in love,
deepen in faith,
and grow in compassion?
Will you carry forward the best of what you bring to one another,
and continue to work on those things with which you struggle,
honoring the work God has accomplished with you?
I will, and I ask God to help me.

F

N., is it your heart's desire and true intent
to enter into the covenant of marriage,
giving of yourself in every way,
with mutual love and respect?
This is my desire and intent.

G

N., do you now desire
to give yourself to N. in marriage?
I do.

H

N., do you now desire
to share your life with N. in marriage?
I do.

I

N., in your baptism
you have been called to union with Christ and the church.
Do you intend to honor this calling
through the covenant of marriage?
I do.

Affirmation of Families/Congregation

Affirmation of the Families

A

To the families of N. and N.,
do you affirm their desire to be married?
We do.
Do you promise to support them
in the life that they will share?
We do.

B

[The minister may address the families of the couple:]
[Names of family members],
do you give your blessing to N. and N.,
and promise to do everything in your power to uphold them in their
    marriage?

[The families of the couple answer:]
We (I) give our (my) blessing
and promise our (my) loving support.
[or]
> **We (I) do.**

[The families of the couple may be seated.]

A
To all who are gathered here,
do you promise to support N. and N.
in their life together?
We do.

B
Do all of you, the family and friends of N. and N.,
pledge to uphold them in their marriage
and encourage them in their life together?
We do.

C
Do you, the family and friends of N. and N.,
promise to encourage them in their marriage,
share in their joy,
and offer your best support and prayers?
We do, and we ask God to help us.

D
Friends and family gathered here,
do you promise to support N. and N.,
as they build a blended family together?
We do.

E
[The minister asks the families:]
Do you, the families of N. and N.,
promise to support and surround them
with your faith, hope, and love?
We do.

[The minister asks the people:]
Do you, the friends of N. and N.,
promise to help and encourage them
in their new life together?
We do.

F

[The minister may address the congregation, saying:]
Will all of you witnessing these vows
do everything in your power
to uphold N. and N. in their marriage?
We will.

Prayer for Illumination

A
Your Word is fresh every day, O God,
like dew on the grass
and manna in the desert.
We come to receive what you offer:
life abundant,
love unending,
a new beginning.

Before we speak our promises
we hear your promise spoken from long ago:
life abundant,
love unending,
a new beginning.

By the power of your Holy Spirit,
illumine our hearts and minds
so that your Word may lead us
into life abundant,
love unending,
and a new beginning that has no end. **Amen.**

B
Holy God,
on this day of celebration
we seek your wisdom.
By the power of your Holy Spirit,
speak to us through your Word,

that we may hear your voice above all others
and know your will for our lives.
In the name of Jesus Christ we pray. **Amen.**

C
God of promise, by your Spirit
help us to listen and find faith
in the story of your saving love
so that we may live more faithfully
as your holy and beloved people;
through Jesus Christ our Lord. **Amen.**

D
Gracious God,
you inspired faithful people to write of your love.
Your Scriptures proclaim the ever-widening call
to love one another and to cherish created life.
Open our ears to the sound of your voice,
that we might hear of your unending faithfulness
and your promise to carry us safely into eternal life,
bound together forever
in the love of Jesus Christ. **Amen.**

E
Almighty God,
illumine our hearts and minds
as your word is read and proclaimed,
so that, by the power of your Holy Spirit,
we may respond in faith.
Perfect your love in us   *1 John 4:16–17*
so that we may abide in you
and love others boldly in your name. **Amen.**

F
Holy God, now send your Spirit
to open our hearts and minds
to the story of your steadfast love for all.
May these words of promise and hope
take root, and grow, and bear good fruit

in the hearts and lives of N. and N.,
and in all of us gathered here,
so that our lives may be made new
by the power of your living Word. **Amen.**

Vows

[Although these vows are newly written, they reflect the content and cadence of marriage vows that have been spoken for centuries.]

A
[The couple join hands; in turn they make their
vows to one another:]

N., where you go, I will go;   Ruth 1:16–17
where you live, I will live;
where you die, I will die;
your people shall be my people,
and your God shall be my God.

I, N., give myself to you, N.,
that we may live in the covenant of marriage,
and I promise,
before God and these witnesses,
to cherish you,
to encourage you,
and to uphold you;
to comfort you in sorrow
and laugh with you in joy,
to remain faithful to you
and nurture my love for you
throughout all our days.

B

N., I promise to love you   *Rom. 12:9–18*
and to honor you,
holding fast to what is good,
and rejoicing in hope.

I promise to be patient in suffering
and to persevere in prayer,
to weep with you when you weep
and rejoice when you rejoice,
now and through all of our days.

C

Who is your beloved?
N. is my beloved.

Do you give yourself to N.
in the covenant of marriage?
I do.

Will you be for N.
a loving and faithful partner
in the life that you share?
I will, with God's help.

D

N., I promise to stand beside you
in adversity and triumph,
through heartache and exceeding joy,
and in the ordinary days of life together.
I promise to encourage you in your endeavors
and in the way of the Lord.
I vow to live in the joy of knowing
you are God's intended gift to me
and, by God's grace,
I will be your *partner/spouse/husband/wife* and companion
for the rest of our days.

E

N., I give myself to you.
Through joys and sorrows,
triumphs and troubles,
in times of plenty and times of want,
I will remain faithful to you
and love you through all of our days.

F

N., I bind myself to you this day
and promise to love you and cherish you,
to support you and comfort you,
to honor you and keep faith with you
as long as we both shall live.

G

N. and N.,
now join hands,
and make your promises to one another.

I, N., promise to love you with my whole heart,
with my imagination, and with my body.
In all things, I promise to understand,
to forgive,
and to take delight in you.
I will keep these promises on good days and on bad,
when I'm confident and when I'm afraid,
when our life together is joyful,
and when our life is difficult.
As I have from the beginning of our relationship,
I will give myself to you with humility and with passion
all the days of our lives.

H

I, N., take you, N.,
to be my love, my partner, my *spouse/husband/wife*;
and I promise
to dwell with you in faithfulness;
to live in the spirit of mutuality,
sharing equally in our common life.

I will support you in times of struggle
and share your deepest hopes
to our life's end.

I
N., my beloved,
I give myself to you—
heart and mind,
body and soul,
now and always.

J
With you, N.,
I will share my life—
all that I am,
all that I have been,
all that I will become.
This I promise.

K
N., you are my beloved,
and I promise,
before God and these witnesses,
to be loving and faithful
in plenty and in want;
in joy and in sorrow;
in sickness and in health;
as long as we both shall live.

L
I, N., take you, N., to be my partner.
All that I am I give to you,
and all that I have I share with you.
Whatever the future holds,
for better, for worse,
for richer, for poorer,
in sickness and in health,
I will love you and stand by you
as long as we both shall live.

M

I, N., take you, N., to be my partner.
All that I am I give to you,
and all that I have I share with you.
Whatever the future holds,
whether sickness or health,
poverty or prosperity,
conflict or harmony,
I will love you and stand by you
as long as we both shall live.
This is my solemn promise.

N

I, N., offer myself to you, N.,
to be your friend, your lover,
your lifelong companion;
to share my life with yours;
to build our dreams together;
to support you through times of trouble,
and rejoice with you in times of happiness.
I promise to treat you with respect, love, and loyalty
through all the trials and triumphs
of our lives together.
This commitment is made in love,
kept in faith, lived in hope,
and eternally made new.

O

I take you, N., to be my partner;
to laugh with you in joy;
to grieve with you in sorrow;
to grow with you in love;
serving humankind in peace and hope;
as long as we both shall live.

Questions and Prayers
for Couples with Children

[Couples who are blending families may choose to make promises to their children. Please see the essay "Couples with Children" on page 188 for thoughts on when this may—or may not—be appropriate.]

A

N. and N., your life together is blessed by children.
Just as you make vows to one another,
you also make promises to your children.

[Have the couple and the children face one another. If the children are sitting in the congregation, have them stand. Have each parent repeat these words to the children of the other parent.]
[Name the children],
Like you, I love your *mother/father* very much.
As I promise to love, respect, and honor *her/him*,
I also promise to love, respect, and honor you.
May our lives together reflect God's love and forgiveness,
and may our home be filled with peace, laughter, and much joy.

QUESTION FOR THE CHILDREN (IF THEY ARE OLDER)
[*Name the children*], your parent(s) seek(s) to build a home
where you are loved in joy and safety;
where you grow in ways that honor your life and gifts;
and where mutual respect is given and received.
Will you do all you can to contribute to the well-being of this family
as your parent(s) enter(s) into marriage this day?
I/We **will.**

QUESTION FOR THE CHILDREN (IF THEY ARE YOUNGER)
[*Name the children*], your parent(s) love(s) you
and want(s) you to be at home in this new family.
Together, they will do all they can to help you grow,
in good times and in hard times.
Do you promise to love them, too,
in good times and in hard times
as you grow together as a family?
I/We **do.**

B

PROMISES AND BLESSINGS BY THE FAMILY
*[When children of previous relationships are being brought into the union,
promises and blessings such as the following may be used. The following
forms may be more useful for older children.]*

[Each parent says to his/her own children:]
[Name(s) of child(ren)],
I promise that my love and care for you
will continue unchanged, as strong as ever.

[Each of the partners says to the other's children:]
[Name(s) of child(ren),]
I promise to welcome you into my life,
to respect you and honour who you are,
to support (*partner's name*) as your *mother/father*,
to care for you, and allow you to care for me.

[The other's children may respond:]
[*Name of partner,*] I/*we* promise to welcome you into *my/our* life,
to respect you and honour who you are,
to support you as *my/our mother's/father's* partner,
to care for you and allow you to care for *me/us*.

[The couple and all the children may say together:]
We make these promises,
trusting not only in our own strength,
but also in the strength of God's love.

[Pastor, addressing each child by name:]
N., you are entering a new family. Will you give to this new family
your trust, love, and affection?
[Each child responds:]
I will, with the help of God.

[Pastor, addressing the couple:]
N. and N., will you be faithful and loving parents to
[names of child(ren)]?

[Couple]
We will, with the help of God.

*[The pastor may invite the immediate families of the couple, including
adults or younger children from previous relationships, to stand in place,
if they are able, and to offer their support in these or similar words.]*

[Pastor, addressing the families:]
Will the families of N. and N. *please stand/please answer* in support of
this couple. Do you offer your prayerful blessing and loving support to
this marriage? If so, please say, "I do."

[Family members]
I do.

*[All family members may be seated. Anyone who escorted the couple may
be seated with their families. The pastor may address the congregation in
these or similar words.]*
Do you, as people of God, pledge your support and encouragement to
the covenant commitment that N.and N.are making together? If so,
please say, "We do."

[People]
We do.

*[An intercessory prayer, using the following or other words, may
be offered.]*

God of our mothers and of our fathers,
hear our pledges encouraging and supporting this union of N. and N.
Bless us as we offer our prayerful and loving support to their marriage.
Bless them as they pledge their lives to each other.
With faith in you and in each other,
may this couple always bear witness
to the reality of the love to which we witness this day.
May their love continue to grow,
and may it be a true reflection of your love for us all;
through Jesus Christ. **Amen.**

D
Merciful God, we thank you for your love
that lives within us and calls us from loneliness to companionship.
We thank you for all who have gone before us.
We thank you for our own parents,
and for all, whether married or single,
who are mother or father to us,
and for countless parents whose names we do not know.
We thank you as we grow to the fullness of the stature of Christ.
Bless N. and N., that they may have the grace
to live the promises they have made.
Defend them from all enemies of their love.
Teach them the patience of undeserved forgiveness.
Bring them to old age,
rejoicing in love's winter more fully than in its springtime.

*[The following words of the prayer may be used if children who will share
in the couple's household are present. If these words are not used, continue
with option A or B of the prayer.]*

Bless *this child/these children*, [*name(s) of children*],
that *he/she/they* may find in this new home
a haven of love and joy where Jesus Christ is honored
in kind words and tender deeds.

1
Finally, in your mercy,
bring N. and N. to that table
where your saints feast forever in your heavenly home;

through Jesus Christ our sovereign Savior who,
with you and the Holy Spirit,
lives and reigns, one God, for ever and ever.
Amen.

2
At the last, receive them and all of us
at the love feast prepared for all the faithful
in your eternal home,
where Jesus Christ,
with you and the Holy Spirit, one God,
reigns in love forever.
Amen.

Blessing of Rings

A
God of infinite love,
bless these rings
and those who wear them,
that they might live together
in harmony and peace;
through Jesus Christ we pray. **Amen.**

B
God of faithfulness and steadfast love,
bless these rings and those who wear them,
that they may be a blessing to one another
and a blessing in your world. **Amen.**

Gen. 12:2

C
O Lord our God, our God alone,
let the promise of your love to N. and N.
be like a sign upon their hands,
that they may love and serve you
with heart, mind, soul, and strength,
and love one another
as Christ has loved us. **Amen.**

Deut. 6:4–9; John 13:34

D
Bless the rings that these hands have worn
these last ___ years.
May they continue to be a visible sign
of their faithfulness,

a circle of eternal love
adorning their daily life. **Amen.**

E
God of steadfast love,
you have given us signs
by which we remember your covenants:
the rainbow,
the stars in the night sky.
In this covenant of marriage,
we bring these rings;
made of strong metals from the earth,
they bend and join,
forming a circle.
Bless these rings, we pray,
that they may be to N. and N.
symbols of the promises
they make this day.
May the strength and humility
of their mutual love
bind and bend them
toward each other,
now and always. **Amen.**

Giving of Rings

A
N., I give you this ring
as a sign of my love,
a pledge of my faithfulness,
and a reminder of the covenant we make this day.

B
N., my beloved,   *Song 2:16*
you are mine
and I am yours.

C
N., I take your hand   *Song 5:4, 16*
and give you this ring.
You are my beloved
and my friend.

D
You, N.,   *Isa. 43:1, 4*
are precious in my sight,
and honored,
and I love you.
I have called you by name;
you are mine.

E
Set me as a seal upon your heart,   *Song 8:6-7*
for love is stronger than death,

and passion more fierce than the grave.
Love flashes like fire, a raging flame.
Many waters cannot quench love,
neither can floods drown it.

F
N., I give you this ring
as a sign of our unending love
and abiding trust.

G
I wear this ring as an everlasting sign
of my love and faithfulness.

H
This ring I give you
as gift and symbol
of our union in marriage;
and of the greater circle of love
in which we are forever known,
and held,
and remembered of God.

I
N., to you
I give this ring:
sign of promise,
gift of love.

J
N., I give you this ring in God's name,
as a symbol of all that we have promised,
and all that we shall share.

Prayer of Blessing

A
Blessed are you, O Lord our God,
for your steadfast love endures forever.
Pour out your blessing upon N. and N.
Uphold the promises they have made
by the power of your living Word.
Fill their hearts and their home
with the gifts of your Holy Spirit.
And by the same Word and Spirit
bless all who are gathered here today
that we may be faithful witnesses
to your great love for all the world;
through Jesus Christ our Savior. **Amen.**

B
Eternal God,
we give you thanks for all the ways you fill our lives with love,
and especially for the love you have given to N. and N.
Bless them in their life together,
that their love for one another may deepen
and their trust in you may grow.

Give them wisdom in their common life
and nurture in them the gift of your grace,
that together they may learn
to love with an everlasting love.
When they hurt one another,
enable them to show mercy.

Cultivate in them a habit of forgiveness,
and lead them into an ever-deepening and mutual self-giving.
Teach them to honor one another in all things
and enable them to keep the vows they have made this day
through whatever joys they share or troubles that befall them.

May this marriage be a gift to all who know N. and N.
Make their life together an expression of your own love for this world,
that in their esteem for one another,
their relationships with neighbors,
and their service to those in need,
all who know them will see a glimpse of your coming reign
of justice, peace, and love.

Bless those gathered here today,
that all who witness these vows
may find their hope renewed
and know the depth of your love and care
for them and for this world you cherish.
All praise to you, triune God,
who created us for love,
became love for the world,
and nurtures love in us all. **Amen.**

C
*[The minister may lay hands on the heads of the couple. In addition, the
assembly may gather around for the laying on of hands.]*
Pour out your Holy Spirit on N. and N.
Continue to give them strength
to live together with love and compassion.
Fill them with genuine delight in one another.
Give them enough creativity to overcome their challenges,
and enough humility to forgive their mistakes.
Grant them patience and generosity,
compassion and tenderness.
Bless their home and make it a place of peace and justice.
Bring your blessing to their waking and sleeping,
to their work and to their play,
to their family and to their friends.

And, at the last, bring them into your eternal home
where all promises will be fulfilled, all wounds healed,
and all gathered in love forever,
through Jesus Christ, our Savior and Light. **Amen.**

D

Gracious God,
because you first loved us,
we are able to love one another.
We thank you for this great gift
that makes all of life deeper, richer,
and more colorful than it might otherwise have been.
We thank you for those who have supported us
and helped us to mature
so that we might be ready for new responsibilities and new
    opportunities.
We remember today those who are not present among us,
and trust that in your great care and keeping,
there is a wider circle of mercy and love
than we ourselves can draw.

We ask, dear God,
that you will especially tend and nurture N. and N.
as they begin their married life this day
and that they[, with their children (*names of the children may be said*)]
will grow in joy and peace and hope.
In their household,
let kindness and gentleness mark their days.
Give them the spirit of forgiveness and patience;
and may joy and laughter be ready companions through the years.
Give them more companions besides—
those who will rejoice or weep with them,
those whose love will be steadfast and sure.

Bless all who have worshiped this day,
that their lives may also be strengthened
for love and by love.
Teach us to recognize
the abundance of all you so freely offer,
so that we may become more generous in a world of need.

Make us lovers and reconcilers and peacemakers,
ambassadors of all your wide and wild purposes.
Because you have welcomed us into your own household,
we, too, will open the doors of our hearts and homes
until your kingdom comes.
In Christ's name, we pray. **Amen.**

E
Eternal God,
without your grace no promise is sure.
Strengthen N. and N. with patience, kindness, gentleness,
and all other gifts of your Spirit,
so that they may continue to fulfill the vows they have made.
Keep them faithful to each other and to you.
Fill them with such love and joy
that they may build a home of peace and welcome.
Guide them by your Word
to serve you all their days.
Help us all, O God,
to do your will in each of our homes and lives.
Enrich us with your grace
so that, supporting one another,
we may serve those in need
and hasten the coming of peace, love, and justice on earth,
through Jesus Christ our Lord. **Amen.**

F
Almighty God,
we thank you for all the ways
love comes into our lives,
and for the opportunities of joy and fulfillment
that marriage brings.

Bless N. and N.,
who have been joined together in your name.
Confirm them in their happiness;
keep them faithful and true to each other,
ready to forgive and be forgiven.
As they grow together in love,
may each be to the other

a companion in joy,
a comfort in sorrow,
and a strength in need.

May your presence in their home
make it a place of welcome and sharing,
of security and peace.
[Bless them with the gift and care of children,
that together they may grow
to know and love you in your Son.]

Bless their families and friends,
who have given them love and friendship
through the years.

We pray for your whole human family,
and for those who suffer while we rejoice.
Bring near the day when all people
will live in peace
and in the knowledge of your love.

Eternal God,
we remember those who were close to us,
who have passed through death
into life everlasting.
Bring us with them at the last
to the Father's house,
the family of God complete
in the glory of your presence;
through Jesus Christ our Lord. **Amen.**

G
[Some or all of the following petitions may be offered.]
Gracious God, we pray for N. and N.
and give thanks that you have brought them together
in this holy union.
Spirit of God,
bless this covenant.

We thank you
for all those whose love has led them
to this day of commitment,
especially for their parents, their friends,
[and their child(ren) N. (and N.),]
those here today and those unable to be here.
Spirit of God,
bless this covenant.

We remember the generations who have gone before us,
[especially . . .]
whom we cannot see, but who are here today in our hearts.
Spirit of God,
bless this covenant.

Help N. and N.
[to be wise and loving *parents/family* and]
to grow together in faithfulness and honesty,
in mutual support and patience.
Spirit of God,
bless this covenant.

Be with them in their work
and renew them in their leisure,
Spirit of God,
bless this covenant.

Make their life together
a sign of your love in this broken world;
may forgiveness heal injury
and joy overcome sorrow.
Spirit of God,
bless this covenant.

May they welcome into their home
both friends and strangers,
and so reflect Christ's love for all people.
Spirit of God,
bless this covenant.

In all their future together,
may they know joy in each other,
and grow through the love they share.
Spirit of God,
bless this covenant. Amen.

H
Eternal God,
Creator and preserver of all life,
author of salvation, and giver of all grace:
look with favor upon the world you have made and redeemed,
and especially upon N. and N.

Give them wisdom and devotion
in their common life,
that each may be to the other
a strength in need,
a counselor in perplexity,
a comfort in sorrow,
and a companion in joy.

Grant that their wills
may be so knit together in your will,
and their spirits in your Spirit,
that they may grow in love and peace
with you and each other
all the days of their life.

Give them the grace,
when they hurt each other,
to recognize and confess their fault,
and to seek each other's forgiveness
and yours.

Make their life together
a sign of Christ's love
to this sinful and broken world,
that unity may overcome estrangement,
forgiveness heal guilt,
and joy conquer despair.

Give them such fulfillment of their mutual love
that they may reach out in concern for others.

[Give to them, if it is your will,
the gift of children,
and the wisdom to bring them up
to know you,
to love you,
and to serve you.]

Grant that all who have witnessed these vows today
may find their lives strengthened,
and that all who are married
may depart with their own promises renewed.

Enrich us all with your grace
that, loving and supporting one another,
we may serve those in need
and be a sign of your kingdom.

Grant that the bonds by which all your children
are united to one another
may be so transformed by your Spirit
that your peace and justice may fill the earth,
through Jesus Christ our Lord. **Amen.**

I
Eternal God,
without your grace no promise is sure.
Strengthen N. and N.
with patience, kindness, gentleness,
and all other gifts of your Spirit,
so that they may fulfill the vows they have made.
Keep them faithful to each other and to you.
Fill them with such love and joy
that they may build a home of peace and welcome.
Guide them by your Word
to serve you all their days.

Help us all, O God,
to do your will in each of our homes and lives.
Enrich us with your grace
so that, supporting one another,
we may serve those in need
and hasten the coming of peace, love, and justice on earth,
through Jesus Christ our Lord.

Eucharist

Eucharistic Prayer A

INVITATION TO TABLE

A

Before the Passover,   *John 13:34–35*
at a meal with his disciples,
Jesus said:
I give you a new commandment,
that you love one another.
Just as I have loved you,
you also should love one another.
By this, everyone will know
that you are my disciples,
if you have love for one another.

This is the Lord's table.
Come and share this feast of love.

B

Hallelujah! The Lord God Almighty reigns.   *Rev. 19:6–9*
Let us rejoice and give glory to God.
The marriage of the Lamb has come.
Blessed are those who are invited
to the marriage supper of the Lamb.

PRAYER OF GREAT THANKSGIVING

*[The structure of this prayer is based on the apostolic benediction
of 2 Cor. 13:13.]*
We give you thanks, O God,
for the abundance of your love.
From generation to generation
you have shown us your faithfulness—
delivering us from captivity,
sending us bread from heaven,
teaching us the wisdom of your way,
leading us toward justice and peace.

Therefore we sing the ancient and eternal hymn:
Holy, holy, holy Lord, God of power and might,
heaven and earth are full of your glory.
Hosanna in the highest.
Blessed is he who comes in the name of the Lord.
Hosanna in the highest.

We give you thanks, O God,
for the grace of the Lord Jesus Christ.
In Christ you came to live among us,
showing your great love for the world—
satisfying our hunger and thirst,
healing our sickness and sin,
sharing our life and death,
rising in glory to reign.

[The words of institution may be included here, if not used elsewhere.]

Remembering your steadfast love,
we offer our lives in love to you.
Remembering your great faithfulness
we proclaim the mystery of faith:
Christ has died,
Christ is risen,
Christ will come again.

We give you thanks, O God,
for the communion of your Holy Spirit.

By the power of your Spirit
be present with us now—
in this bread and this cup,
in this gathering of your people,
in the company of all believers,
in a world so hungry for love and grace.
Make us ready for that great feast
at the marriage of heaven and earth
and the birth of your new creation.

Keep us in the grace of the Lord Jesus Christ,
in the abundance of your love, O God,
and in the communion of your Holy Spirit,
now and forever. **Amen.**

Eucharistic Prayer B

SETTING THE TABLE
*[An offering may be collected for the work of the church or to support a
cause that is important to the couple. Bread and wine may be set on the
table and Communion prepared.]*

PRAYER OF GREAT THANKSGIVING
The Lord be with you.
And also with you.
Lift up your hearts.
We lift them to the Lord.
Let us give thanks to the Lord our God.
It is right to give our thanks and praise.

It is indeed right, our duty and our joy,
that we should at all times and all places
give our thanks and praise to you, gracious God,
through our Savior Jesus Christ.
At the wedding in Cana in Galilee
Jesus turned water into wine,
making marriage a sign of a glory that is yet to come.
With great joy, with our whole lives,
and with all the saints,
we praise your name and join their unending hymn:

Holy, holy, holy Lord, God of power and might,
heaven and earth are full of your glory.
Hosanna in the highest.
Blessed is the one who comes in the name of the Lord.
Hosanna in the highest.

Holy mystery,
energy that powers the universe,
your Word set creation into motion:
ever-expanding, evolving, multiplying, flourishing.
You brought human life out of primordial mist,
setting us in this garden home,
instilling in us the capacity to love,
endowing us with the imagination
to form friendships and make love.
We heard you tell our ancient parents
that it is not good to be alone
and command them to fill the earth with blessing.

Yet, so often, we were afraid.
We failed to nurture your good creation.
We limited the wideness of your love
by pretending that some are loved by you,
and others are outside your grace.
Again and again, you sent men to remind us of mercy,
and women to demand justice.

At the right time, you sent Jesus,
an open channel of light and love,
who turned water into wine,
rejection into welcome,
hunger into fullness,
and death into life.

On the night after a woman
anointed his feet with perfumed oil,
the night of his own suffering and betrayal,
Jesus gathered with friends and washed their feet.
He took bread, gave thanks, broke it,
and gave it to them, saying:

Take and eat; this is my body, given for you.
We do this to remember that we are his body.

After the meal, he took a cup of wine,
gave thanks, and shared it for all to drink, saying:
This cup is the sign of a new covenant,
offered to the whole creation
that sins might be forgiven
and love restored.
We do this to remember that we share his life.

Remembering his promise to be present
whenever we gather at this table,
let us proclaim the mystery of faith:
Christ has died.
Christ is risen.
Christ will come again.

At this table
pour out your gentle Spirit,
turning this marriage celebration into heaven,
this bread and wine into holy food,
and this assembly into a community of love that never ends.
Amen. Come, Holy Spirit.

To you, Holy God,
our source, our light,
our bread, our life,
our water and our wine,
we give you praise,
without reserve,
without end. **Amen.**

Gathered by the Holy Spirit, let us pray as Jesus taught us . . .

[The assembly prays the Lord's Prayer.]

BREAKING OF THE BREAD
Reveal yourself to us in the breaking of the bread,
as you once revealed yourself to the disciples.

Make this cup a sign of great celebration
as when you once turned water into wine.

These are the gifts of God for the people of God.
Thanks be to God.

COMMUNION OF THE PEOPLE

PRAYER AFTER COMMUNION
Jesus Christ,
friend and lover,
we give you thanks for joining us in this celebration.
Now that we have feasted on your glory
and have known your mercy,
pour us out for the sake of the world,
that all might know this love
and be drawn into a community of justice. **Amen.**

Lord's Prayer

A

Our Father in heaven,
hallowed be your name,
your kingdom come,
your will be done,
on earth as in heaven.
Give us today our daily bread.
Forgive us our sins
as we forgive those who sin against us.
Save us from the time of trial
and deliver us from evil.
For the kingdom, the power,
and the glory are yours
now and forever. Amen.

B

Our Father, who art in heaven,
hallowed be thy name,
thy kingdom come,
thy will be done,
on earth as it is in heaven.
Give us this day our daily bread;
and forgive us our debts,
as we forgive our debtors;
and lead us not into temptation,
but deliver us from evil.
For thine is the kingdom,
and the power, and the glory forever. Amen.

C

Our Father, who art in heaven,
hallowed be thy Name,
thy kingdom come,
thy will be done,
on earth as it is in heaven.
Give us this day our daily bread.
And forgive us our trespasses,
as we forgive those who trespass against us.
And lead us not into temptation,
but deliver us from evil.
For thine is the kingdom,
and the power, and the glory, forever and ever. Amen.

The Peace

A

Live in peace, *2 Cor. 13:11*
and may the God of love and peace
be with you.
And also with you.

B

The grace, mercy, and peace of God *2 Tim. 1:2; 2 John 1:3*
be with you all.
And also with you.

C

May mercy, peace, and love *Jude 1:2*
be yours in abundance,
now and forever.

D

Jesus came to his own disciples, *John 20:19–21*
whose doors were locked in fear.
Peace be with you, he said,
sending them out
to live in perfect freedom,
witnesses of the good news.
This day, we are sent out
with Jesus' own breath on our faces:
"Peace be with you."
And also with you.

E
The peace of Christ be with you always.
And also with you.

[The assembly may greet one another with a sign of peace.]

Declaration of Marriage

A

N. and N. are married. *Heb. 13:4*
Let their marriage be held in honor by all.

B

N. and N., you are married. *Rom. 8:38–39*
Now hear and believe this good news:
There is nothing in life or in death;
nothing in the past, present, or future;
no power in heaven or on earth,
nor anything else in all creation
that will ever be able to separate you
from the love of God in Jesus Christ our Lord.
Thanks be to God!

C

N. and N. have made promises to one another
in the presence of God and this assembly
and have sealed those promises with the giving and receiving
    of rings.
Let their marriage be held in honor by all.

D

Having made their promises before God and this assembly
and given public witness to their commitment,
N. and N. are now married in the state of ___ [in the eyes of
    God and the church].
Those whom God has brought together, let no one separate.
Thanks be to God.

E

By the vows made this day
in the presence of God and this community,
I declare that N. and N.
are now joined in the covenant of marriage.
In the household of faith,
we rejoice with them [and their children]
on this glad occasion,
and celebrate with joy
their life together.

F

[The couple join hands, and the minister says:]
Let us pray.
Wise and loving God, by your providence
you have brought N. and N. together.
Now, in the mystery of your grace,
let them be united as one.
Let the life they now share
be a sign of your new creation,
a source of new and abundant life,
and a gift of love for all the world;
in your holy name we pray. **Amen.**
[The minister announces the marriage:]
N. and N., you are now married.
Let all that you do be done in love.   *1 Cor. 16:14*
[The couple may kiss.]

Charge to the Couple

[The minister may charge the couple.]

A

As God's own, holy and beloved,   *Col. 3:12–14*
clothe yourselves with compassion,
kindness, humility,
meekness, and patience.
Bear with one another,
forgiving each other
just as the Lord has forgiven you.
Above all, clothe yourselves with love,
which binds everything together
in perfect harmony.

B

May the God of peace   *1 Thess. 5:23–28*
make and keep you
holy and whole—
body, mind, and spirit—
until Christ comes in glory.
God is faithful;
God will do this.
Now, beloved, greet one another
with a holy kiss.
[The couple may kiss.]
The grace of the Lord Jesus Christ
be with you all. **Amen.**

C

Stand firm in your faith.   *1 Cor. 16:13–14, 20, 23*
Be courageous and strong.
And let all that you do
be done in love.
Now greet one another
with a holy kiss.

[The couple may kiss.]

The grace of the Lord Jesus Christ
be with you all. **Amen.**

D

May the Lord direct your hearts   *2 Thess. 3:5*
in the love of God
and the faithfulness of Christ. **Amen.**

E

May you grow in the grace and wisdom   *2 Pet. 3:18*
of the Lord and Savior Jesus Christ,
to whom we give all glory
now and forever. **Amen.**

F

May peace and love   *Eph. 6:23–24*
and grace and faith
be with you all.
And also with you.
The love of Christ
will never end.
Thanks be to God.

G

Let love be genuine;   *Rom. 12:9–13, 18*
hate what is evil, hold fast to what is good;
love one another with mutual affection;
outdo one another in showing honor.
Do not lag in zeal, be ardent in spirit, serve the Lord.
Rejoice in hope,

be patient in suffering,
persevere in prayer.
Contribute to the needs of the saints;
extend hospitality to strangers.
If it is possible, so far as it depends on you,
live peaceably with all.

H
The commandment we have had from God   *2 John 1:5–6*
from the beginning is this:
let us love one another.
And this is love:
that we walk according to God's word and ways.
As we go from this place,
where love has been promised, professed, and sealed,
let us practice love
steadfastly and abundantly!

I
Hear the words of Paul to the gathered faithful
    in Philippi:
Finally, beloved,   *Phil. 4:8–9*
whatever is true,
whatever is honorable,
whatever is just,
whatever is pure,
whatever is pleasing,
whatever is commendable,
if there is any excellence
and if there is anything worthy of praise,
think about these things.
Keep on doing the things
you have learned and received
and heard and seen in me,
and the God of peace will be with you.

J
As God's own,   *Col. 3:12–14*
clothe yourselves with compassion,
kindness, and patience,

forgiving each other
as the Lord has forgiven you,
and crown all these things with love,
which binds everything together in perfect harmony.

Benediction

[The minister may give a blessing to the couple and the congregation.]

A

The Lord bless you and keep you.   *Num. 6:24–26*
The Lord be kind and gracious to you.
The Lord look upon you with favor
and give you peace.
Alleluia! Amen.

B

May the holy Trinity,   *1 Cor. 13:13*
God of faith,
God of hope,
God of love,
bless and keep you
now and always.
Alleluia!

C

[This option combines peace, charge/kiss, and blessing.]
May the God of love and peace be with you.   *2 Cor. 13:11–13*
And also with you.
Now greet one another with a holy kiss.
[The couple may kiss.]
The grace of the Lord Jesus Christ,
the love of God,
and the communion of the Holy Spirit
be with you all. **Alleluia!**

157

D
May the grace of Christ attend you,
the love of God surround you,
and the Holy Spirit keep you,
this day and forevermore. **Amen.**
[The couple may seal their vows with a kiss.]

E
The God of creation,
who made you and delights in you;
the Christ of incarnation,
who redeemed you and befriends you;
the Spirit of power,
who gives you life and passion;
bless you now and for the rest of your days. **Amen.**

As a testimony to your promises and your love,
you may kiss one another.

F
The love of God,
the grace of Christ,
and the peace of the Holy Spirit
fill you this day
and forever.

G
In wilderness and promised land,
God be with you;
on the way of discipleship,
the grace of Christ attend you;
and for all that is to come,
the joy of the Spirit guide you,
today and all your days.

H
May the God of every blessing   *1 Cor. 13:13*
keep you in faith, hope, and love
today, tomorrow, and forever.

I

The grace of Christ attend you,
the love of God surround you,
the Holy Spirit keep you,
that you may live in faith,
abound in hope,
and grow in love,
both now and forevermore.

J

May the Holy and Eternal One—   *Rev. 4:8*
who was and is and is to come—
bless and keep you, now and always.

K

May the One who makes all things new   *Rev. 21:5, 22–27*
write your names in the book of life
and shine on you with endless light.

❧ *Hymns* ❧

"A Hymn in Praise of God's Love"

Michael Morgan   *SLANE**

Your love above us, unmeasured, always;
source of our being, and heir of all praise;
call us to worship; reach down and embrace;
lead us in wisdom, bind us through your grace.

Your love within us, so tender, so strong,
lightens our darkness, turns sadness to song;
hope and compassion, and faith to believe;
ours for the giving, and ours to receive.

Your love around us, so boundless and true;
give us a yearning to be more like you.
Hold and enfold us, our strength to the end,
sharing and caring for partner and friend.

Your love beside us, in hearts that adore;
lives joined together, more rich than before;
vows heard and spoken, deep blessings conferred;
bound by a promise, and sealed in God's word.

*Sung to the tune of "Be Thou My Vision."

"Rejoice in Christ the Lord! (In Love Abide)"

David Gambrell

DARWELL'S 148TH*
John 15:1–17

Rejoice in Christ the Lord!
your new life has begun:
united by the grace of God,
the Three-in-One.
In love abide—
rejoice, and let the God of love
be glorified!

Have faith in Christ the Lord,
whose mercy never ends:
no longer only servants, now
beloved friends.
In love abide—
have faith, and let the God of love
be glorified!

Bear fruit in Christ the Lord,
the vine in whom we grow:
bear witness to the God from whom
all blessings flow.
In love abide—
bear fruit, and let the God of love
be glorified!

*Sung to the tune of "Rejoice, the Lord is King."

Go forth in Christ the Lord!
This is the gospel call:
to give as you receive, and show
God's grace to all.
In love abide—
go forth, and let the God of love
be glorified!

"From Sacred Love"*

Mary Louise Bringle   LM†

From sacred Love, all loving flows—
the mystic white and perfect rose
that guides our journeys, once begun,
and moves the gleaming stars and sun.

Naomi, well beloved of Ruth,
heard from her lips this loyal truth:
"Where'er thou goest, I will go.
Thy people shall be mine also."

Like Jonathan at David's side,
or Mary, Joseph's promised bride,
love blooms in variegated flowers
when watered by the Wellspring's powers.

To Jesus, his beloved friend
stayed faithful to the trying end.
So we commit, eternally,
all that we have, all we can be.

Creator, Christ, and Holy Ghost,
and all the bright angelic host,
now dance with joy and mystic round,
where sacred Love on earth is found.

†Often sung to the hymn tune called WALY WALY, which is the tune often used for "The Water is Wide" and "Though I May Speak with Bravest Fire." Another common tune for this text is MARYTON ("O Master, Let Me Walk with Thee"). However, it may be sung to any Long Meter tune.

"Love Has Brought Us Here Together"*

Mary Louise Bringle

8787 D HYFRYDOL†
Texts: Song of Solomon 2:4 and 8:6–7
1 Corinthians 13:4–7

Love has brought us here together:
love of family, love of friends;
love, our vow till death should part us;
love, God's gift, that never ends.
From our birth, throughout our lifetime,
love's insistence calls our name.
Floods of waters cannot drown it,
or put out its dancing flame.

Love is gentle, love is patient,
soft in words and kind in deeds.
Never pompous or self-centered,
love puts first the other's needs.
Not quick-tempered or resentful,
prone to take offense or brood,
love excels in grace and mercy,
never jealous, never rude.

Love does not rejoice at evil;
love rejoices in the right.
Keen in giving and forgiving,
spreading love is love's delight.
When two people pledge their union,
all who witness are renewed,
feasting at love's earthly banquet,
tasting heaven's beatitude.

†Often used for "Come, Thou Long-Expected Jesus" and "Love Divine, All Loves Excelling."

166

Prayers for Particular Occasions

Engagement

A
God of new beginnings,
you have caused your love to grow
between N. and N.
As they begin to imagine their future together,
fill them with delight and joy.
Give them strength and patience
for the planning ahead.
Most of all, let them experience the coming days
as holy and treasured time.
In Jesus' name. **Amen.**

B

[It would be especially appropriate to lead this prayer at the baptismal font, with the couple joining hands over the water.]
Holy, triune God—
fountain of blessing,
river of redemption,
ocean of love—
you call us to be holy;
you call us to be one.

We give you thanks for N. and N.
and for the commitment they have made
to live their lives together
as people you have
chosen, claimed, and called
in Jesus' name.

[The minister may pour water over the hands of the couple, still joined.]
Pour out your grace upon them now.
Help them to prepare
for their new life together
with all the blessings and challenges,
joys and struggles they will face.

Help all of us
to support and surround them with love
as we look forward
to that great and joyful day
when these two will become one.
In your holy, triune name we pray. **Amen.**

C
Loving God,
we celebrate and give thanks for the engagement of N. and N.
We are grateful for their mutual love;
for the honor and respect they show to one another.

Bless this time of preparation for marriage.
Give them your wisdom and strength as they plan,
and space to dream beyond the details.
Weave joy and gladness in and through
their conversations and considerations
and grant them patience with one another
when they are overwhelmed,
so that the days ahead may
prepare the way for a fruitful life together.
In Christ's love, we pray. **Amen.**

Rehearsal Dinner

A

God of blessing,
pour out your Spirit on this meal.
Bless family and friends that have gathered from near and far.
Renew relationships,
heal old wounds,
and create new bonds of family
that bind all of us more closely together.
May the friendships and family that we create
bring new blessing and peace to the world around us.
We pray in Jesus' name. **Amen.**

B

God of our ancestors,
all the families of the earth are one in you.

We give thanks that you have gathered us
at this common meal, this joyful feast,
to celebrate the gift of your love to N. and N.
and to savor the promise of their life together.

As you nourish us with this food,
strengthen and sustain them for the journey ahead
so that they may share the fullness of life
that you alone can provide;
through Jesus Christ, our daily bread. **Amen.**

C
Loving God,
from whom all blessings flow.
As we prepare to share this wonderful feast
we pause to give you thanks for many gifts.

For the lives of N. and N.,
whose love for one another
reflects your light that shines in the darkness;
may these moments with them inspire all here
to seek that light and share it with others.

For supporting families and friends,
who have nurtured and now surround N. and N. with their love;
may they feel appreciated for all their loving care.

For those here working to serve us
as we celebrate this special day;
bless them and their families
and lead them safely home when their work is done.

For food planted, grown, harvested, and graciously served;
may your earth and those who farm it
be treated with dignity and justice.

Nourish us with this food.
Create in us a spirit of peace.
Guide our feet to do your will,
to the glory of your holy name.
In Jesus Christ we pray. **Amen.**

D
With abundant joy at this abundant feast,
we give thanks to you, Creator God.
You have blessed us with gifts of the earth that nourish us
and gifts of love that make us glad.
As we anticipate the marriage of N. and N.
and join in their celebration,

we ask your blessing upon all gathered here
and upon those who prepared this meal.
With gratitude for your many provisions,
we lift up our hearts to you, O God,
the source of all life and the fount of all love. **Amen.**

Gathering of the Wedding Party
before the Service

[This prayer might be used before a wedding rehearsal (often the day before the wedding) and/or before the wedding itself.]

A
God of endless love and grace,
we give you thanks for N. and N.,
and for the mystery of your providence
that brought them to this place
of commitment, of challenge, of care.

Pour out your peace among us now
as we prepare for this great celebration.

Calm our restless minds,
soothe our anxious spirits,
and fill our hearts with your presence,
so that we may proclaim with joy
the wonder of your saving love;
through Jesus Christ our Lord. **Amen.**

B
God of love,
for so long, we have planned and dreamed about this day.
Fulfill our hopes,
and bring your great love to this wedding.
As we enter into worship,
give us a sense of peace and calm.
We know that all things are held in your loving hands.

Grant that this day will end in blessing,
and that the life that N. and N. will share will glow with happiness.
In Jesus' name we pray. **Amen.**

C
Gracious God,
as we prepare to worship you
prepare us for this special moment.
Calm our nerves.
Center our minds.
Cast out distracting thoughts.
Help us focus on your loving presence
as we witness promises made,
through Jesus Christ we pray. **Amen.**

D
Go before us, God, we ask.
Calm our nerves even as you increase our joy.
We surround N. and N. with our presence
and with promises of our own
to love and support them in their life together.
We are witnesses to your grace this day:
how love believes, hopes, and endures all things   *1 Cor. 13:6–7*
and rejoices in the truth.
Lead us out now, dear God,
in joy and peace. **Amen.**

Couple Getting Married Elsewhere

A
Lord Jesus Christ,
our companion on the road,
we commend to your care
our friends N. and N.
who go now to be married.

Walk beside them, O Lord—
not only in this journey,
but all along the way of life
that stretches out before them.

Though we may not travel with them,
help them to know and trust
that we will stand beside them
through all the days to come.

Keep them in our hearts and prayers
until they return to us again,
and we may celebrate together
the new life they have begun.

All this we ask, O Lord,
in your holy name. **Amen.**

B
God of the Promised Land,
your people have often crossed borders
in search of freedom and abundant life.

Even when their journey was challenging,
you blessed them along the way
with your sure presence to sustain and to guide.

As N. and N. continue their journey together,
anticipating their longed-for marriage,
they travel now with great joy to a place
where vows will be said,
and rings exchanged,
and their love sealed with honor.

Surrounding them with affection and respect,
we entrust their journey to your care and provision,
and anticipate their return with joy.
Our family [community]
is enriched by the love they share with us
and the ways they reflect your light to the world.
O God, keep their going out and their coming in,   *Ps. 121:8*
now and forever. **Amen.**

Reception

A

God of celebration,
the authors of Scripture proclaim
that God's presence is best known
when we gather around tables to celebrate family and community.
May this marriage banquet feed us, not just with good food,
but with friendship and joy.
May N. and N. be blessed in the years ahead
with many reasons to feast and to toast their joy.
Bring your blessing now to this celebration,
that we might be strengthened to feed the world
with good food and abundant joy.
In the name of Jesus we pray. **Amen**.

B

*[This prayer was written for a pastor to pray at a reception after the
couple was married in a civil union, but it might also be used in Sunday
worship when the congregation recognizes and celebrates a marriage that
has taken place elsewhere (e.g., courthouse, another church, different
state, destination wedding).]*
Loving God,
we give you thanks for N. and N.,
and for the love
that has brought them together.

We give you thanks
for the promises they have made,
to you and to one another.

We give you thanks
for the community that surrounds them,
offering support and care.

Above all, we give you thanks
for the grace of Jesus Christ,
in whom we all are bound together
as your beloved children.

Receive our prayers for N. and N.

By your steadfast love,
strengthen them in faithfulness
to you and to one another.

Let their lives together
be filled with wonder.

In times of struggle,
give them hope and courage;
in times of joy,
give them gratitude and praise.

Bless and keep them always,
and let them be a blessing to others—
a sign of your gracious love for all;
in Jesus' name we pray. **Amen.**

C
Faithful God, we praise you for the gift of love
that we have witnessed in the marriage of N. and N.

Bless them each day with your goodness and grace
so that they may be a blessing in your world.

Bless the meal we are about to share,
so that we may be nourished in faith, hope, and love.

Let the sweetness of this celebration
remain in our hearts and on our lips

until that joyful day when we meet again
at the marriage feast of heaven and earth;
through Jesus Christ our Savior. **Amen.**

D
Loving God,
in the glad company of family and friends
we celebrate the marriage of N. and N.
Thank you for this time of music, laughter,
conversation, and joy.
With lightness of spirit,
send them dancing into their life together today.
With fullness of heart,
shower them with peace in all the years to come.
With love unending,
surround them and all gathered here,
now and forever. **Amen.**

Anniversary

A

God of the journey,
through the years, you have walked with N. and N.
You have provided them with laughter and joy,
and given them strength and courage in times of trouble.
Continue to bless their life together,
that their love might find new depths
and lead them around surprising corners.
May their love unearth their deepest integrity,
that in their union, they might truly find
whom God has created them to be.
Bless them in the years ahead,
and on the last day
bring them into the joy of heaven,
where love will never end.
In the name of Jesus Christ we pray. **Amen.**

B

God of steadfast love and faithfulness,
we give you thanks for N. and N.
and for the life and love they share.

We celebrate all the good things
you have done in their lives.

We bear witness to your presence with them,
even through hurt and hard times.

We look forward, with hope and joy,
to the future that lies before them.

As you have blessed them with your love,
continue to bless and keep them, now and always;
through Jesus Christ, Alpha and Omega. **Amen.**

C
Gracious God,
we give thanks for promises made and promises kept;
for the covenant of marriage sustained over time;
and especially for the love that N. and N.
have shared for ___ years.

By your grace they have continued to abide in love,
in joy and in sorrow,
in sickness and in health,
in times of plenty and in times of want.

The circle of their life together has increased,
including those gathered here, and many others besides.
Bless and redeem their memories of the years that have passed,
sustain them in their common life today,
and give them good hope for the years to come.

As you are faithful in your covenant with us,
so help us to be faithful to you
as we serve one another and all of creation.
In Christ's name, we pray. **Amen.**

PART 3

❧ PRACTICAL CONCERNS ❦

Interfaith Weddings

There is no one way to plan an interfaith wedding. Some faith traditions have formal rules prohibiting clergy from performing or participating in interfaith marriage ceremonies. Other traditions give clergy some discretion in deciding their level of participation in interfaith weddings. In still other traditions, there is an open embrace of interfaith ceremonies. Couples interested in a marriage service that honors both of their faith traditions will want to speak to their respective clergy to determine what is possible. Ideally, wedding services should be planned by representatives from each participating faith. It may serve the couple well to include families in this discussion, too. Often families have stronger feelings about religious choices than do the couple. Planning an interfaith marriage ceremony can be an exercise in understanding and preparing for differing family traditions and religious practices. Tensions can often be present around holidays, life transitions, and home faith practices. The wedding planning process can be a way of discussing these issues.

Before the 1960s, interfaith unions accounted for about 20 percent of marriages, but between 2000 and 2010, 45 percent of marrying couples were interfaith unions. Despite this increase, fully interfaith marriage ceremonies are not the norm: More than half of all interfaith couples were married by a wedding officiant from only one religion; 43 percent had a civil ceremony in which clergy were not involved. In only 4 percent of interfaith weddings did clergy from two different faiths participate.*

Some traditions provide guidelines for interfaith celebrations. The concept of *respectful presence* is encouraged in Christian relationships with

*These statistics are from Naomi Schaefer Riley, *'Til Faith Do Us Part: How Interfaith Marriage Is Transforming America* (New York: Oxford University Press, 2013), cited in Celeste Kennel-Shank, "Mixed and Matched: Challenges of Interfaith Weddings," *Christian Century*, May 28, 2014, 28.

persons of other religions. Respectful presence "offers Christians a way to participate [in celebrations that include a variety of faiths], expressing respect for persons of other faiths while maintaining loyalty to the Christian gospel." Indeed, respectful presence "is a way to follow Jesus of Nazareth, who met with people of many cultures and religions even as he fulfilled the nature and purpose of his God-given mission."* Christian leaders may want to pay special attention to this issue of respect. Religious leaders from minority faith traditions often have experienced the assumption by Christian ministers that Christianity is the norm. This may shape how they will participate or plan for an interfaith ceremony. Care should be taken so that symbols or practices from other religions do not seem secondary to Christian practices, even if the latter may have risen to the level of cultural expectation.

While some interfaith couples choose to be married in a civil ceremony and others choose to hold two separate wedding services following the cultural and religious traditions of each, still others seek an interfaith marriage service. There are two basic forms for interfaith weddings; ideally, the services should be planned with representatives from each participating faith.

1. In the marriage service, language and symbols acceptable to both faith traditions are incorporated. This form is not intended to water down either faith tradition. In fact, care is taken to ensure that the participants may pray together authentically and the respective faith traditions are expressed with integrity. Symbols are often helpful in finding common ground for the service. For instance, symbols such as light or flame and strands of cord may be common to both faith traditions, and these symbols can be incorporated authentically and effectively into the marriage liturgy.† Couples may be surprised to learn that the deep pattern of marriage rituals has some profound consistencies across time and place.

2. In the marriage service, the two faith traditions use language and symbols that are distinct to each particular tradition. In this service, couples and participants seek to stand with one another in prayer. There are alternating moments in the wedding service when one faith tradition prays fully or performs a ritual that is distinct to that tradition in the presence of others, while persons of the other faith tradition observe with respectful attention.

*"Guidelines for Interfaith Celebration of Thanksgiving," in *Book of Occasional Services: A Liturgical Resource Supplementing the Book of Common Worship, 1993* (Louisville, KY: Geneva Press, 1999), 285.
†See Kennel-Shank, "Mixed and Matched," 28–29.

In each of these two forms of interfaith weddings, there is a common understanding that this occasion of interfaith celebration is not to be used as an opportunity for conversion. Care is also taken to ensure that neither faith dominates the other in the service itself.

Couples with Children

Many couples come to marriage with one child or more, having raised children together before coming to marriage or bringing children from previous relationships. A wedding can be an opportunity to celebrate the commitments of the new family, especially for couples whose children are still growing up. Acknowledging children as part of a new family can be pastorally helpful in creating or strengthening ties between parents and children. Deciding how and even whether to involve a child in the wedding depends upon the age of the child, the child's attitude toward the marriage, and the couple's relationship to the child. A child of any age, even an adult child, may be ambivalent or resistant to accepting a new parent, and a member of a couple may be struggling to accept a partner's child from a previous relationship.

Children under Six

If the marriage ceremony is public confirmation of a long-established relationship the child has always known and enjoyed, the child will probably be very happy and excited, because this act only solidifies a loving relationship between two people in the child's life. Many children in this situation will wish to participate in some way, perhaps as a ring bearer or flower girl. However, children under the age of six are unpredictable, and even ordinarily well-behaved children may act out in the midst of the excitement and stress of a wedding. A child who successfully fulfills a role at the wedding rehearsal may become confused or upset when faced with the reality of walking down an aisle with strangers watching. Since the focus in the wedding should be on the couple and not the child, perhaps a trusted member of the extended family or an adult friend the child knows well can be with her or him during the ceremony. The couple's vows to each other in the ceremony might be followed by promises to care for the children, and prayers might include petitions for the children. Children might be brought to their parents at this point in the ceremony, underscoring the family ties, but all involved need to be prepared to adapt in the moment to a child's unexpected response.

A couple bringing children who have been raised by just one parent into a new blended family should be especially careful with children under six. Children may not understand the significance of the wedding, but they will definitely be aware that something big is happening that they cannot control. They are not able to articulate their feeling of insecurity that someone else is going to have Mommy or Daddy's attention, but they surely will be feeling it. Special care from the primary parent should be taken to assure children of their place, while acknowledging that things will change.

Children Six to Twelve

Children ages six through twelve are better able to understand the significance of a wedding. A child who is pleased and even excited about the marriage will probably welcome an acknowledgment of his or her part in the new family. Not only might the couple promise to care for the child, the child might also reciprocate with a statement or an affirmative response to a question about the child's acceptance of the new family. Care must be taken, however, to prepare statements that children and adults can say with integrity, rather than insisting that a person, whether child or parent, make promises that do not feel genuine (see below). A prayer for the new family might acknowledge the reality of new bonds even when there is ambivalence or resistance. Standing together for a statement of commitment and prayers will visually reinforce the establishment of new family ties. Some children may relish the idea of serving as a flower girl or ring bearer as well, while others will want to avoid the limelight.

Teenagers

When teenagers are part of the family, particular sensitivity is needed. At this developmental stage, a teen's peers become more significant than the parents, and it may be difficult for a teen to accept a new parent while trying to establish an identity separate from parents. Yet teens also need the stability of family life, and for most teens it will be important to recognize their place in the new family even if they appear disinterested or resentful. Teenagers are able to think more abstractly than younger children, making it possible to involve them in decisions about what they will say and where they will stand during the ceremony.

Statements of the parents' commitment as well as the teen's acceptance of a new parent can be an important affirmation of a teen's place in the new family system, and prayers for parents as well as for the teenager can acknowledge both the blessings and challenges of family life. If the parents have been raising the child together for several years, a teenager might offer a statement of blessing and support. In every case, it is important that these statements express the sincere commitments of the speakers.

Grown Children

Grown children will relate to a marrying couple as adults. A couple's decision to involve grown children in the wedding ceremony depends on their relationship and the children's attitudes toward the marriage. An adult child might present a parent for marriage or serve as an attendant at the wedding, rather than make a statement of commitment.

Should Children Make Promises at a Wedding?

Parents and pastors should think carefully about whether children of any age should, even if eager and willing, make a promise to the parents as part of the marriage ceremony. What happens later if the couple decides to separate? Will the child's promises be taken into account?

One alternative is to encourage children to participate in the wedding as a sign of their commitment, perhaps as ushers, attendants, ring bearers, or readers of Scripture. They have an opportunity to verbally express their approval when the family and/or the entire congregation affirms its support of the couple. In this case, the couple is still encouraged to make promises to support the child as part of their promise to one another. A sign of this promise, such as a necklace or pin, might be given to the children.

Same-Gender Weddings

As same-sex marriage has become possible in parts of church and society, many gay and lesbian couples are tying the knot. This is the first generation of young same-sex couples who can get married just like their heterosexual friends. At the same time, many older couples have been together for years and now can seek both the privileges and protections of the state and also the blessing of their church.

All weddings have the potential for drama and stress as extended families and friends come together to celebrate the new union. Due to the discrimination and prejudice they have faced, some added potential challenges can surface for same-gender couples. Ministers can help allay stress and avoid difficulty by talking with couples about some or all of these issues.

— Many gay and lesbian Christians have a love-hate relationship with the church. The same church that loved them as children and taught them the Christian faith later rejected them as they became aware of their sexual orientation. Some may have faced public scorn and ridicule. All heard messages of condemnation and shame, no matter how subtle. To ask for the church's blessing may seem to some like seeking an abused parent's love. The two people marrying may not agree on the importance of the church's blessing.

— Many left the church that condemned them in order to survive and live as the people God made them to be. Some held on to the faith taught to them and continued to develop spiritually outside of organized religion. As a result, some couples may exemplify a very strong, albeit nontraditional, faith. They may wish to use in their weddings particular symbols or words that sustained them when the church did not. Clergy steeped in traditional church liturgies can listen to the couple's wishes and honor what is behind their desires while planning a worship service that respects all.

— Many long-term couples have already held a wedding or holy union service in a church or another setting, despite the lack of legal or church sanction. Now that marriage is permitted, they may seek a church blessing on their relationship. Some may prefer a full-blown wedding ceremony so that they may invite family and friends who did not attend before. In this case, it is appropriate to acknowledge in the service that the couple are affirming vows they have already made. Others may prefer to honor their initial wedding but desire a renewal or reaffirmation of vows at a church that now recognizes them.

— Same-gender couples who have been out a long time have already gone through the drama of losing friends and close family members who did not accept them. For many, that separation was dramatic and scarring. The question of whom to invite to the wedding may reopen wounds that have only partially healed. Should parents who have cut them off be invited? What if one partner has an accepting family and the other does not? Should the accepted partner have the right to push the other to invite her estranged family? How can the accepting family be supportive? Weddings do offer the possibility of grace. Estranged friends and family may decide to attend and by their presence offer a gesture of repentance and love. However, a couple must be prepared for the possibility that some whom they invite will choose not to come. When making the guest list, each couple will need to carefully consider how to balance their hopes for reconciliation with the possibility of renewed hurt.

— Family members will also have to deal with their own feelings and relationships. A wedding may present a new opportunity for families to keep score of who will approve, or not approve, of the nuptials. When families are bitterly divided, they risk facing the scorn of those who disagree with their decision to attend or not attend. It is hoped that all who choose to attend would be ready to affirm the marriage and celebrate with the couple, though even a relative who cannot quite support the marriage, but nevertheless makes the effort to attend, should be made welcome.

At weddings of gay, lesbian, bisexual, or transgender people, there may be many who have experienced the church as hurtful and judgmental. The welcome is an opportunity to speak a new word that many may have not heard from the clergy. These words of welcome can be an important announcement of the gospel of love that Christians know in Jesus Christ. Following are some examples:

A

Sisters and brothers, all are welcome in this place. The church has not always been a place where we have been able to gather and hear the blessing of God. Yet today we celebrate here the love that welcomes everyone, regardless of whom we love, where we have been, what we believe, or what we have done. Today, love is at the center, and God makes us into a family of blessing that gives light to the world.

B

In the name of Jesus Christ, I welcome you to this place. Today, we celebrate that our *nation/state/city* now offers its recognition and surrounds N. and N. with the communal support that honors and binds them together. From many backgrounds and many beliefs, we gather to witness to the wide and wonderful diversity of God's creation.

C

Today we celebrate that love wins: the love of God, the love of N. and N., and the love of this gathered assembly for them. We celebrate that our *nation/state/city* now offers the rights and privileges that should have been offered all along. We know that God has blessed them all along. Now, we give thanks that God moves us, and the whole world, into deeper and wider patterns of love. We give thanks for the diversity of this gathering and pray that our love for one another will change the world.

Music at Weddings

Music makes a celebration. As long as humans have gathered in groups to commemorate important events in the life of an individual or community, we have been singing and chanting, drumming and dancing, playing pipes and strumming strings. Music has a way of gathering us together, lifting us out of the ordinary, carrying the weight of deep emotion, getting our hearts in tune and synchronizing our actions, giving substance to what is sacred, and expressing things that words alone cannot convey.

So music is a critical component of a meaningful marriage service. This is about so much more than filling dead airtime while guests gather or providing a suitable soundtrack for the happy day. Music has a powerful part to play, an instrumental role—forming the community that will bear witness to the couple's vows and support them in their life together; establishing a sense of wonder, joy, solemnity, and celebration; expressing the faith, hope, and love of the two people who are joined in marriage and the families that surround them; inspiring worshipers to show such love in their own relationships and daily lives; and sharing the great story of God's saving love for all.

When planning music for a wedding, there are many important factors to consider. If the service will take place at a church, be respectful of the musical staff in that congregation and honor the gifts they bring. Ask their advice, learn from their experience, respect their limits, be mindful of their schedules, and pay them generously. When working with other musicians, particularly for services in locations other than a church, be sure they understand the shape and substance of the marriage liturgy and are prepared to offer their gifts in the spirit of worship. Otherwise, all the same things apply: treat them professionally and compensate them fairly.

Let instrumental music underscore the action of worship, and not undermine it. Consider the rhythm, tempo, and tone of each piece and ask whether it contributes to the action of the liturgy or distracts from it. If an instrumental piece has words associated with it, think about the associations those words might convey in the minds of worshipers, even when the words are not sung. Use instrumental music in a meaningful way, not merely as a cover for silence.

Bear in mind the importance of congregational singing at a communal event such as a wedding. As suggested above, music shapes the community and provides a way for all to participate in the action of the service. Let the people sing, and give them songs that will help them express their faith, hope, love, and support for the couple. Use soloists sparingly, and only in ways that contribute to the service of worship and give voice to the whole assembly's prayer and praise. Let everything be done for the glory of God.

Classic Hymns

"Come, Thou Fount of Every Blessing," Robert Robinson; NETTLETON
"Deck Yourself, My Soul, with Gladness," Johann Franck, trans. Catherine Winkworth; SCHMÜCKE DICH
 "Joyful, Joyful, We Adore Thee," Henry van Dyke; HYMN TO JOY
"Love Divine, All Loves Excelling," Charles Wesley; BEECHER or HYFRYDOL
"More Love to Thee, O Christ," Elizabeth Payson Prentiss; MORE LOVE TO THEE
"Now Thank We All Our God," Martin Rinkart, trans. Catherine Winkworth; NUN DANKET
"O Love That Wilt Not Let Me Go," George Matheson; ST. MARGARET
"Praise the Lord! God's Glories Show" (Psalm 150), Henry Francis Lyte; LLANFAIR

Symbols Used in the Wedding Service

The primary symbols are already present in most marriage rites: gathering of an assembly, making promises, exchanging rings, and blessing of the new marriage. The most significant, of course, is the making of promises. When two people turn to one another, holds hands, and look into one another's eyes to make a promise of love and commitment, the assembly witnesses the heart of the ritual. In fact, it could be argued that anything that precedes or follows supports and highlights this fundamental act. Any other rituals should focus on this primary symbol, rather than detract from it.

Other significant ritual elements in the marriage rite point to the central act of making promises. Family and friends may offer their prayers and support through their own rituals of promise making. Rings may be passed through the assembly, with each person holding them in blessing before handing them on and bringing them forward. The couple might be taken to the center of the room, allowing those gathered to surround them in blessing. The laying on of hands, often part of the pastoral blessing following the promises, may be joined by the entire assembly, each person placing a hand on the shoulder of a person near them. Members of the assembly may be given their own candles, a flame spreading through the assembly from a marriage candle as a sign that all share in the support of this new marriage. These sorts of communal actions may take place either before the making of promises or after the marriage announcement.

Increasingly, marriage includes family members from previous marriages. It may be appropriate for families to make special promises to one another. One spouse may promise to care for another's children. Children may promise to embrace this new family. Care should be taken to use ritual language that has integrity, making sure that all parties are making promises that they genuinely desire to make. It is particularly important that children not be coerced into expressing support for new family configurations.

Children from previous relationships or spouses who are becoming parents for the first time may have deep ambivalence or even resistance to this new family arrangement.

Pastors must exercise sensitivity when planning these moments. Simply standing together may be enough of a symbolic act. It may be appropriate to include a visual element that signifies the making of this new family. Pouring different colors of sand in layers or placing a variety of flowers in a vase could serve to emphasize each person's individuality as well as point to the new family that is created by the marriage. Children may give a new parent a flower, or the new parent may promise to love and care for the child, offering an affectionate gesture. Children who are ready and eager to participate should be encouraged to see themselves as vital actors in this new creation.

In most rites, there is some kind of announcement of the marriage by the officiant following the making of promises and exchanging of rings. At this point it may be appropriate to incorporate other meaningful or culturally significant rituals. The lighting of a unity candle, jumping a broom, placing of crowns, presentation of floral necklaces, or other culturally specific rituals make most sense at this time in the service. Again, care should be taken that any of these additions not overshadow the primary act of making promises.

Since same-sex marriage is now legal in the United States, it may be important for some couples to include the signing of the marriage license during the service. This may come after the pastoral announcement in order to make clear that the state is a witness to this marriage, not the source. Including the marriage license in the liturgy may depend on the theological understanding in the tradition. Care should be taken that the signing is done with theological and ritual integrity.

Increasingly, the marriage liturgy is home to creative interpretations and rituals. People come to their marriage services with a variety of traditions and expectations. The rite is simple enough to embrace this beautiful diversity. Any additional symbols should not only express the character of the couple, but also honor the primary pattern of gathering, promise making, blessing, and sending.

Walking Down the Aisle

Somehow, some way, the entire wedding party, including the presider and the couple, need to get to the front and center of the worship space. The traditional method involves several male friends and possibly groomsmen serving as ushers and escorting people to their seats, ending with key family members such as grandparents and parents. The groomsmen then take their place with the groom and minister at the front and the procession begins. The bridesmaids march, glide, or sashay down the aisle, and finally the father of the bride walks the bride to the front and hands her over to the groom before sitting down in the front row with her mother.

Many adaptations have been made to this traditional model, based on necessity. Perhaps the father of the bride is deceased. Perhaps there are two brides or two grooms. Or the attendants for each spouse are not just one gender. There is no one right way to do this! While the point is simply to get the guests to their places and the couple and the wedding party in their places, a few guidelines are useful:

— Help people get seated, especially those needing assistance. Sometimes friends of each spouse are to sit on a particular side, and guests will want to know where they should be seated. In other cases, couples prefer to have guests sit wherever they would like. Ushers can give this guidance.
— Honor those who have played a central role in raising the spouses. Although no one needs to "give away" the bride like a piece of property, it is appropriate to give special attention to key people like parents and grandparents.
— Avoid treating genders differently and furthering stereotypes. A bride may choose to have a best man, for instance, or women may serve

as ushers. Attendants may enter the worship space together in any configuration.

Some adaptations may include:

— Have the entire wedding party process to the front, in whatever configuration works best (groomsmen with bridesmaids, groomsmen followed by bridesmaids, groomsmen and bridesmaids coming down separate aisles or together—the possibilities are endless). Each person coming to be married may be accompanied by her or his family. Once down front, the families may sit down or they may stand behind the spouses as the presider gives words of greeting and purpose. An acknowledgement of support may be asked of the families, who then take their seats.
— If children are involved and comfortable, have them walk with each parent and stand by their parent during the ceremony or take a seat once they are down front.
— Have both genders serve as ushers. It is best that the couple not serve as ushers only because it might be difficult to manage conversations and begin the service on time.

Scripture Suggestions

When two people are married in a Christian service, Scripture holds a prominent place. Suggestions follow for biblical passages that may be proclaimed in the reading and preaching of the Word. Some texts refer to the praise of God or the love of Christ; others speak about the calling of Christians or disciplines of the Christian life.

Then the LORD God said, "It is not good that the man should be alone; I will make him a helper as his partner." So out of the ground the LORD God formed every animal of the field and every bird of the air, and brought them to the man to see what he would call them; and whatever the man called every living creature, that was its name. The man gave names to all cattle, and to the birds of the air, and to every animal of the field; but for the man there was not found a helper as his partner. So the LORD God caused a deep sleep to fall upon the man, and he slept; then he took one of his ribs and closed up its place with flesh. And the rib that the LORD God had taken from the man he made into a woman and brought her to the man. Then the man said, "This at last is bone of my bones and flesh of my flesh; this one shall be called Woman, for out of Man this one was taken." Therefore a man leaves his father and his mother and clings to his wife, and they become one flesh. (Gen. 2:18–24)

But Ruth said, "Do not press me to leave you or to turn back from following you! Where you go, I will go; Where you lodge, I will lodge; your people shall be my people, and your God my God." (Ruth 1:16)

When David had finished speaking to Saul, the soul of Jonathan was bound to the soul of David, and Jonathan loved him as his own soul.

Saul took him that day and would not let him return to his father's house. Then Jonathan made a covenant with David, because he loved him as his own soul. Jonathan stripped himself of the robe that he was wearing, and gave it to David, and his armor, and even his sword and his bow and his belt. (1 Sam. 18:1–4)

Thus Jonathan made a covenant with the house of David, saying, "May the LORD seek out the enemies of David." Jonathan made David swear again by his love for him; for he loved him as he loved his own life. (1 Sam. 20:16–17)

The following psalms expressing joy and thanksgiving are often used:

67
95
100
103:1–5, 15–18
121
136:1–9, 26
150

Two are better than one, because they have a good reward for their toil. For if they fall, one will lift up the other; but woe to one who is alone and falls and does not have another to help. Again, if two lie together, they keep warm; but how can one keep warm alone? (Eccl. 4:9–11)

The voice of my beloved!
    Look, he comes,
leaping upon the mountains,
    bounding over the hills.
My beloved is like a gazelle
    or a young stag.
Look, there he stands
    behind our wall,
gazing in at the windows,
    looking through the lattice.
My beloved speaks and says to me:
"Arise, my love, my fair one,
    and come away;

for now the winter is past,
the rain is over and gone.
The flowers appear on the earth;
the time of singing has come,
and the voice of the turtledove
is heard in our land.
The fig tree puts forth its figs,
and the vines are in blossom;
they give forth fragrance.
Arise, my love, my fair one,
and come away.
(Song 2:8–13)

Set me as a seal upon your heart,
as a seal upon your arm;
for love is strong as death,
passion fierce as the grave.
Its flashes are flashes of fire,
a raging flame.
Many waters cannot quench love,
neither can floods drown it.
If one offered for love
all the wealth of one's house,
it would be utterly scorned.
(Song 8:6–7)

When Jesus saw the crowds, he went up the mountain; and after he sat down, his disciples came to him. Then he began to speak, and taught them, saying:
"Blessed are the poor in spirit, for theirs is the kingdom of heaven.
"Blessed are those who mourn, for they will be comforted.
"Blessed are the meek, for they will inherit the earth.
"Blessed are those who hunger and thirst for righteousness, for they will be filled.
"Blessed are the merciful, for they will receive mercy.
"Blessed are the pure in heart, for they will see God.
"Blessed are the peacemakers, for they will be called children of God.
"Blessed are those who are persecuted for righteousness' sake, for theirs is the kingdom of heaven." (Matt. 5:1–10, the Beatitudes)

"You are the salt of the earth; but if salt has lost its taste, how can its saltiness be restored? It is no longer good for anything, but is thrown out and trampled under foot.

"You are the light of the world. A city built on a hill cannot be hid. No one after lighting a lamp puts it under the bushel basket, but on the lampstand, and it gives light to all in the house. In the same way, let your light shine before others, so that they may see your good works and give glory to your Father in heaven." (Matt. 5:13–16)

"Everyone then who hears these words of mine and acts on them will be like a wise man who built his house on rock. The rain fell, the floods came, and the winds blew and beat on that house, but it did not fall, because it had been founded on rock. And everyone who hears these words of mine and does not act on them will be like a foolish man who built his house on sand. The rain fell, and the floods came, and the winds blew and beat against that house, and it fell—and great was its fall!" (Matt. 7:24–27)

And one of them, a lawyer, asked him a question to test him. "Teacher, which commandment in the law is the greatest?" He said to him, "'You shall love the Lord your God with all your heart, and with all your soul, and with all your mind.' This is the greatest and first commandment. And a second is like it: 'You shall love your neighbor as yourself.' On these two commandments hang all the law and the prophets." (Matt. 22:35–40)

"But from the beginning of creation, 'God made them male and female.' 'For this reason a man shall leave his father and mother and be joined to his wife, and the two shall become one flesh.' So they are no longer two, but one flesh. Therefore what God has joined together, let no one separate." (Mark 10:6–9)

On the third day there was a wedding in Cana of Galilee, and the mother of Jesus was there. Jesus and his disciples had also been invited to the wedding. When the wine gave out, the mother of Jesus said to him, "They have no wine." And Jesus said to her, "Woman, what concern is that to you and to me? My hour has not yet come." His mother said to the servants, "Do whatever he tells you." Now standing there were six stone water jars for the Jewish rites of purification, each holding twenty or thirty gallons. Jesus said to them, "Fill the jars with water." And they filled them up to the brim. He said to them, "Now draw some out, and take it to the chief steward." So they took it. When the steward tasted the water that had become wine, and did not know where it came from (though the servants who had drawn the water knew), the steward called the bridegroom and said to him, "Everyone serves the good wine first, and then the inferior wine after the guests have become drunk. But you have kept the good wine until now." Jesus did this, the first of his signs, in Cana of Galilee, and revealed his glory; and his disciples believed in him. (John 2:1–11)

"As the Father has loved me, so I have loved you; abide in my love. If you keep my commandments, you will abide in my love, just as I have kept my Father's commandments and abide in his love. I have said these things to you so that my joy may be in you, and that your joy may be complete.

"This is my commandment, that you love one another as I have loved you. No one has greater love than this, to lay down one's life for one's friends. You are my friends if you do what I command you. I do not call you servants any longer, because the servant does not know what the master is doing; but I have called you friends, because I have made known to you everything that I have heard from my Father. You did not choose me but I chose you. And I appointed you to go and bear fruit, fruit that will last, so that the Father will give you whatever you ask him in my name. I am giving you these commands so that you may love one another." (John 15:9–17)

For I am convinced that neither death, nor life, nor angels, nor rulers, nor things present, nor things to come, nor powers, nor height, nor depth, nor anything else in all creation, will be able to separate us from the love of God in Christ Jesus our Lord. (Rom. 8:38–39)

I appeal to you therefore, brothers and sisters, by the mercies of God, to present your bodies as a living sacrifice, holy and acceptable to God, which is your spiritual worship. Do not be conformed to this world, but be transformed by the renewing of your minds, so that you may discern what is the will of God—what is good and acceptable and perfect. (Rom. 12:1–2)

Let love be genuine; hate what is evil, hold fast to what is good; love one another with mutual affection; outdo one another in showing honor. Do not lag in zeal, be ardent in spirit, serve the Lord. Rejoice in hope, be patient in suffering, persevere in prayer. Contribute to the needs of the saints; extend hospitality to strangers.

Bless those who persecute you; bless and do not curse them. Rejoice with those who rejoice, weep with those who weep. Live in harmony with one another; do not be haughty, but associate with the lowly; do not claim to be wiser than you are. Do not repay anyone evil for evil, but take thought for what is noble in the sight of all. If it is possible, so far as it depends on you, live peaceably with all. (Rom. 12:9–18)

If I speak in the tongues of mortals and of angels, but do not have love, I am a noisy gong or a clanging cymbal. And if I have prophetic powers, and understand all mysteries and all knowledge, and if I have all faith, so as to remove mountains, but do not have love, I am nothing. If I give away all my possessions, and if I hand over my body so that I may boast, but do not have love, I gain nothing.

Love is patient; love is kind; love is not envious or boastful or arrogant or rude. It does not insist on its own way; it is not irritable or resentful; it does not rejoice in wrongdoing, but rejoices in the truth. It bears all things, believes all things, hopes all things, endures all things.

Love never ends. But as for prophecies, they will come to an end; as for tongues, they will cease; as for knowledge, it will come to an end. For we know only in part, and we prophesy only in part; but when the complete comes, the partial will come to an end. When I was a child, I spoke like a child, I thought like a child, I reasoned like a child; when I became an adult, I put an end to childish ways. For now we see in a mirror, dimly, but then we will see face to face. Now I know only in part; then I will know fully, even as I have been fully known. And now faith, hope, and love abide, these three; and the greatest of these is love. (1 Cor. 13:1–13)

As many of you as were baptized into Christ have clothed yourselves with Christ. There is no longer Jew or Greek, there is no longer slave or free, there is no longer male and female; for all of you are one in Christ Jesus. (Gal. 3:27–28)

[Unfortunately, the following Scripture has often been used to justify a patriarchal pecking order in heterosexual marriage rather than a focus on the selfless love both partners should show one another. The text in its original context was a refreshing and liberating word to women in a male-dominated *world. The author here tells Christian men to give themselves up for their wives as Jesus did for others. After centuries of misusing this liberating text to preach women's second-class position, some preachers today may enjoy recovering the original message of the text, which is relevant to any relationship serious about following Jesus.]*

Be subject to one another out of reverence for Christ.

Wives, be subject to your husbands as you are to the Lord. For the husband is the head of the wife just as Christ is the head of the church, the body of which he is the Savior. Just as the church is subject to Christ, so also wives ought to be, in everything, to their husbands.

Husbands, love your wives, just as Christ loved the church and gave himself up for her, in order to make her holy by cleansing her with the washing of water by the word, so as to present the church to himself in splendor, without a spot or wrinkle or anything of the kind—yes, so that she may be holy and without blemish. In the same way, husbands should love their wives as they do their own bodies. He who loves his wife loves himself. For no one ever hates his own body, but he nourishes and tenderly cares for it, just as Christ does for the church, because we are members of his body. "For this reason a man will leave his father and mother and be joined to his wife, and the two will become one flesh." This is a great mystery, and I am applying it to Christ and the church. Each of you, however, should love his wife as himself, and a wife should respect her husband. (Eph. 5:21–33)

Rejoice in the Lord always; again I will say, Rejoice. Let your gentleness be known to everyone. The Lord is near. Do not worry about anything, but in everything by prayer and supplication with thanksgiving let your requests be made known to God. And the peace of God, which surpasses all understanding, will guard your hearts and your minds in Christ Jesus.

Finally, beloved, whatever is true, whatever is honorable, whatever is just, whatever is pure, whatever is pleasing, whatever is commendable, if there is any excellence and if there is anything worthy of praise, think about these things. Keep on doing the things that you have learned and received and heard and seen in me, and the God of peace will be with you. (Phil. 4:4–9)

As God's chosen ones, holy and beloved, clothe yourselves with compassion, kindness, humility, meekness, and patience. Bear with one another and, if anyone has a complaint against another, forgive each other; just as the Lord has forgiven you, so you also must forgive. Above all, clothe yourselves with love, which binds everything together in perfect harmony. And let the peace of Christ rule in your hearts, to which indeed you were called in the one body. And be thankful. Let the word of Christ dwell in you richly; teach and admonish one another in all wisdom; and with gratitude in your hearts sing psalms, hymns, and spiritual songs to God. And whatever you do, in word or deed, do everything in the name of the Lord Jesus, giving thanks to God the Father through him. (Col. 3:12–17)

So we have known and believe the love that God has for us.
God is love, and those who abide in love abide in God, and God abides in them. (1 John 4:16)

Sermon Ideas

A

Ruth 1:16–17. Even though this story is about a mother-in-law and her daughter-in-law, it presents a model of faithfulness. Here two people—women—bind themselves to each other for the sake of their shared future, in hope and mutual care, courage and creativity. And from their commitment to each other, a new family becomes possible.

B

Psalm 133. The psalmist uses vivid imagery to give thanks for unity. When families and friendships are fractured and alienated over attitudes regarding sexual orientation, this psalm could give voice to the family that gathers in unity and joy for the marriage.

C

Psalm 139. This psalm acknowledges that we are created and fashioned by God just as we are—and God knows and loves us in just this way. That same God promises to be with us in every circumstance—in plenty and want, joy and sorrow, sickness and health.

D

Matthew 5:3–12. A sermon on the Beatitudes can offer blessing and signal the coming of justice to those who have been denied the right to marry.

E

John 2:1–11. According to the Gospel of John, the first sign of Jesus' glory was revealed at a wedding feast in Cana. John 2:1–11 tells the story of Jesus turning ordinary water into fine wine, an indication of rich extravagance and deep abundance of God's grace in our everyday lives. This text also points to the hope we have in the coming reign of Christ. The sign Jesus performs at Cana is just the first of many—the initial glimpse of his glory, which we will one day know in full. Marriage, too, can sometimes give us a glimpse of glory, a foretaste of the whole and complete love we will enjoy when Christ comes again.

This would be an especially appropriate text for preaching at a wedding that included the Lord's Supper.

F

Romans 12:9–18. Paul's guidance to the church is also good advice for couples entering into marriage, and for all who seek peace, harmony, and love in their home, congregation, neighborhood, and world. Read in the context of a wedding, this text has both an inward turn, instructing two people how to live well with one another, and an outward turn, urging the couple to allow their marriage to be a source of blessing to others.

G

1 Corinthians 12:12–31. We often read 1 Corinthians 13 ("love is patient; love is kind") at weddings. But the passage immediately before it, 1 Corinthians 12:12–31, has profound things to say about human life in relationship. Beginning with baptismal imagery, this passage teaches how we are called to live together as members of one body through both suffering and joy.

H

Colossians 3. This text offers the image of "clothing." Often at weddings, people have put much thought, time, and planning into what they will wear—they want everything to be perfect! The preacher might point to the kind of effort, thought, and care that goes into the spiritual "clothing" for the rest of the married life that follows the wedding day. This passage describes how being baptized in Christ enables us to clothe ourselves in his love and compassion. Those who would marry (and indeed, people in all sorts of relationships) are able to offer their love because they are clothed in his.

Sacraments and Weddings

A sacrament is a sacred act of the church, instituted by Jesus Christ, in which God's grace is communicated or conferred through word, action, and prayer. In some Christian traditions (Roman Catholic, Orthodox, Anglican), marriage is considered to be a sacrament. In many Protestant denominations this is not the case. Some hold that only baptism and the Lord's Supper are sacraments instituted by Jesus Christ because they are the only acts the Bible says he performed.

Nevertheless, there are significant ways in which Christian marriage is related to the sacramental life of the church and its members. Through baptism, we enter a covenant relationship with God, are incorporated into Christ's body, and receive the gifts of the Holy Spirit. Marriage is also a covenant relationship, in which two people become one flesh and share the gifts they have received. At the Eucharist (Communion or Lord's Supper), we give thanks for the grace of God, celebrate the mystery of Christ's saving love, and are sent to show the life of the Spirit in the world. Marriage is also a relationship in which we practice a life of gratitude, are nourished with love, and are called to love and serve others. For these reasons, it can be highly appropriate and deeply meaningful to include elements of sacramental celebration in the service of Christian marriage.

There are a variety of ways to point to the connection between the covenant of baptism and the covenant of marriage. The minister might begin the service by pouring water into the font at the opening sentences or call to worship, invoking the name of the triune God who is the source of all love. The couple being married might pause at the font to touch the water on their way to the front of the worship space, remembering the journeys of faith that have brought them to this place. The minister might lead the confession and pardon at the font, lifting water at the declaration of forgiveness as a sign of cleansing and renewal, as the life of marriage requires frequent forgiveness and constant grace. The couple might stand at the font to speak their vows, remembering the promises made at their baptisms. Indeed, it would be appropriate for the entire wedding liturgy to take place around the baptismal font.

In the same way, it is appropriate to conduct part or all of the marriage service at a place near the Communion table. Among other things, being married means meeting at table and sharing regular meals. In the church's liturgy as in daily life, eating together is an intimate encounter, a holy thing. Just as the church remembers and celebrates its union with Christ in the Lord's Supper, couples and families nourish and strengthen their relationships each time they share a common meal. If the church's Communion table is ordinarily at the front and center of the worship space, resist the temptation to move it to make room for the wedding party; rather, let the table stand where it is as a vivid symbol of the common life this couple will now share.

In some traditions, it is typical for weddings to conclude with the Eucharist—a sacramental sign of covenant commitment, self-giving relationship, and mutual service and love. If you plan to include the Lord's Supper in a marriage service, think carefully about pastoral implications. Consider the faith commitments of the couple, as well as the family and friends who will attend. Will all (or most) be able to receive the sacrament with integrity and joy? Remember that some Christian traditions do not share "full communion." Will members of other churches—or people of other faiths, or those with no religious tradition—feel excluded? Be clear in communicating invitations and expectations—whether in a verbal announcement, a bulletin note, or both—remembering that friends or family members may have little or no relationship with your sacramental tradition or experience of Christian worship. If Communion is served, give explicit instructions about how the elements are to be received, and provide a graceful way for some to opt out, perhaps by remaining in their seats or by coming forward to receive a word or gesture of blessing.

Sometimes a couple will want to share in Communion as the first act of their marriage, but will not wish to extend the sacrament to all present. This is an impulse to be avoided; Eucharist is a common meal, the meal of all the baptized, and not a private celebration. If a couple is to take part in the sacrament, then all Christians who are present are to be invited to the Table.

Lightning Source UK Ltd.
Milton Keynes UK
UKOW06f0614010616

275379UK00007B/204/P